The Art of J. D. Fergusson

THE ART OF J.D. FERGUSSON

A Biased Biography
by
Margaret Morris

My father was a farmer
  Upon the Carrick Border,
And carefully he bred me
  In decency and order;
He bade me act a manly part,
  Though I had ne'er a farthing,
For without an honest, manly heart,
  No man was worth regarding.
Robert Burns

Blackie: Glasgow and London

Published with the assistance of the Scottish Arts Council

Copyright © 1974 Margaret Morris

0 216 89708 4

Blackie & Son Limited
Bishopbriggs, Glasgow G64 2NZ
5 Fitzhardinge Street, London W1H 0DL

Printed in Great Britain by Robert MacLehose, University Press, Glasgow
Filmset by Thomson Litho, East Kilbride, Scotland

I dedicate this book
on Fergus's behalf
to his parents
John and Christina Fergusson

Colour Plates

Paintings in Text

Contents

I am deeply indebted to

JEAN GEDDES

a painter who knew Fergus.

She has done the research for me
and also deciphered and typed
his letters and notes
usually written in pencil.

FOREWORD

When Margaret Morris invited me to write a foreword to this book, I addressed her in my reply as "M.M." and she subsequently asked me to call her "Meg" as Fergusson did, and to call him "Fergus" as his friends did. But to use either of these terms would have made me feel presumptious. I called him "J.D." We were never on intimate terms. Intimacy is something I have always instinctively avoided. I recognised in J.D. a great artist as the little group of his closest friends did—but, for far too long a time, who else? I had known of him for a long time before we met. I referred to the way he had been neglected in my *Contemporary Scottish Studies* (1926) and I was a subscriber to *Rhythm* the little magazine which, along with Estelle Rice, he edited at the instigation of Middleton Murry and Katherine Mansfield. But I did not meet him till the early 1940s when he was actively engaged with the New Art Club in Glasgow along with Andrew Taylor Elder, the Hannah brothers, James Burns Singer the poet, Professor Andrew McLaren Young, Donald Bain, Dr. Tom Honeyman and others. What appealed to me so strongly in him was just that quality which makes the choice of Burns's verse on the flyleaf of this work so absolutely right. I do not think what differentiates

J.D. from most Scottish painters today can be better put than he put it when he wrote: 'By painting I mean using oil paint as a medium to express the beauty of light on surfaces. What we used to call in Scotland "quality of paint"—with solidity and guts—not drawing a map-like outline and filling in the spaces with an imitation of the colour of the object with the paint. That is the difference between the "Glasgow School" paintings and Academic paintings. I try to describe it as the difference between Harris tweed, composed of all sorts of colours in wool, and any cheap material dyed one flat colour. Even threadbare Harris tweed still has colour, luminosity and durability, and probably looks better when worn—I think so.

Margaret Morris does well in this wonderful book to quote this passage from the tribute of an old friend of J.D.'s early Paris days, André Dunoyer de Segonzac:

'Ce grand artiste, d'une totale indépendance, a ignoré les formules éphèmeres du moment et a suivi sa voie durant sa longue et belle vie d'artiste. Son veuvre subira victorieuse-ment l'épreuve du temps car elle ẽt authentique, très vivante et vraie.'

In my autobiography, *Lucky Poet* I have said I am sure I could not fail to meet any man or woman, alive during my lifetime, with whom I had much in common. So it was inevitable that, though late in the day, I should meet J.D. Margaret Morris tells me that J.D. would have wanted me, rather than anyone else, to write this foreword. But good wine needs no bush. Little known though J.D. may have been in his lifetime this book more than makes up for that now. It is one of the best books devoted to any Scottish artist. In just the same way as my meeting with J.D. was inevitable, so with the many overlapping friendships recounted in these pages—Eric de Banzie, Billy McColl, John Ressich, David

Anderson and many others whom I knew mutually with
J.D. and M.M.

I was privileged to speak at a memorial dinner to J.D., and
I cannot do better now than quote what I said then about the
very essence of his genius as an artist: "There has never been
more need of art than today. This ought to be the great hour
of the artist. Many men have dimly realised from the
beginning that the Poet is our only Priest. Today it is more
than a dim realisation. For what other saviours have we now?
We turn to the Scientist to solve the riddle of the universe:
and he hands us back a *formulated* riddle. We turn to the
old-time Philosopher and he speaks to us at great length upon
all that is known, only to tell us in the end that that which we
want to know is beyond understanding. We turn to the
Priest: and—most times—we turn away. We turn to the
Artist. He does not reply. Nor seeks he to assert, nor argue,
nor explain, nor advise. He holds up a piece of reality—See!
He gives no commands. He pronounces no judgment. He
offers no consolation. He simply *reveals*."

> "Disputation through Logic,
> speculation through Philosophy,
> investigation through Science—
> revelation through Art."

'For after all', wrote Havelock Ellis, communicating with the
ageless seer across the centuries, 'we cannot go beyond the
ancient image of Heraclitus, the "Ever-living Flame, kindled
in due measure, and in like measure extinguished". That
translucent and mysterious Flame shines undyingly before
our eyes, never for two moments the same, and always
miraculously incalculable, an ever-flowing stream of fire.
The world is moving, men tell us, to this, to that, to the other.
Do not believe them! Men have never known what the

world is moving to. Who foresaw—to say nothing of older and vaster events—the Crucifixion? What Greek or Roman in his most fantastic moments prefigured our thirteenth century? What Christian foresaw the Renaissance? Who ever really expected the French Revolution? We cannot be too bold, for we are ever at the incipient point of some new manifestation far more overwhelming than all our dreams. No one can foresee the next aspect of the Fountain of Life. And all the time the Pillar of that Flame is burning at exactly the same height it has always been burning at!'

It burned beautifully in J.D. and its full effulgence is caught in these pages.

Hugh MacDiarmid

SCOTLAND
1874 ~ 1905

I first met Fergusson in 1913, when I took my dancers to Paris to appear at the Marigny theatre. Armed with an introduction, I presented myself at his studio at about four in the afternoon. The door was opened a few inches and a dripping black head appeared and said—"I mean to say . . . I'm in my bath, can you come back in half an hour?"

Fergusson had already lived in Paris eight years, since 1905, and had many friends by this time. They called him Johnny and he wore an emerald green tie (which I still have). When he appeared in a café they would chant a parody of a popular song of the day, 'Anybody here seen Kelly':

> Anybody here seen Johnny
> J O double N Y;
> Anybody here seen Johnny,
> Johnny with the green neck tie;
> His hair is black and his eyes are blue
> And he's a Scotsman through and through,
> Anybody here seen Johnny
> Johnny with the green neck tie?

I thought Johnny was much too ordinary a name for such a striking personality and when he explained to me that Fergusson must be spelled with two S's because it meant the son of Fergus, and that King Fergus came from Ireland and settled in Scotland, it seemed obvious that he must be descended from King Fergus and so I called him Fergus. And as he did not like the name Margaret, he said he would call me Meg. From then on we were known to our friends as 'Fergus and Meg'.

Fergus refused to pay any attention to birthdays. He said it was much better not to know how old you were—it was how well you felt and what you did that mattered. He thought he was born in March. I was born March 10th, so we were both Pisces and both adored the sea. One day I had a letter from the Tate Gallery, who had one of Fergus's pictures, asking me the place and date of my husband's birth. I had to reply that I did not know. About two weeks later I received another letter saying "It may interest you to know that your husband was born at Leith on March 9th, 1874."

I think Fergus would have liked to have been born in the Highlands, but his father and mother left Pitnacree in Perthshire for Leith just before his birth. From time to time he told me his memories of childhood and I shall relate them.

There was a wonderful old Highland nurse who brought up the whole family. Fergus was the oldest, then followed two sisters, and finally his brother Robert, about twelve years his junior. Fergus's first impression of his father was his reading aloud in the evenings, and himself crawling under his knees and round his legs, and sitting on his feet, so he must have been pretty small. Later he learned it was mostly the Old Testament, or poems of Robert Burns that were read. Something must have got through, for Fergus liked to read me passages from Job or the Song of Solomon, and Burns's poems.

14

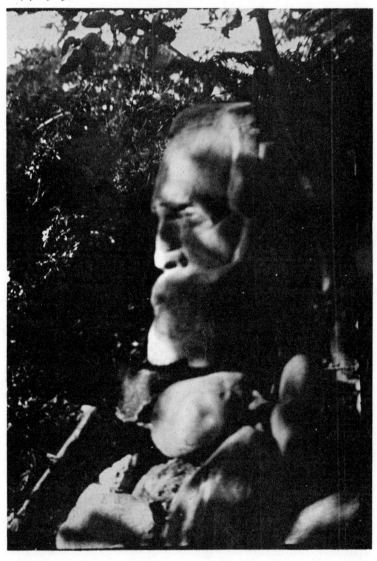

While the family were still at Leith, Fergus was taken to a small 'Dame School'. He remembered vividly his dislike of being kept in a room at a desk instead of out of doors, and he persisted in looking through the window instead of at the blackboard, so spent much time standing on a form with a pointed dunce's hat on. He preferred that, he said, to doing lessons. Even at that early age, he was so convinced he was right in feeling it was better to look at nature than at a blackboard that he felt no shame when laughed at. Standing on the form, he could still see the branches of the trees and the birds through the window.

He must have learned a little at that school, because the next story he told me could only have been a few years later. His parents were very hard up and certainly could not entertain, but one day, probably through the school he attended, he received a formal invitation to a party.

'. . . requests the company of Master Fergusson etc. . . .'

His mother explained that he must write a formal acceptance and put a piece of paper in front of him. He read the invitation carefully and then wrote across the middle of the notepaper—

'Master Fergusson doesn't want to go'.

Though the form of refusal was doubtless modified, it is to his mother's credit that she did not try to make him accept.

Some years later his family left Leith and moved to the outskirts of Edinburgh. Fergus was sent to the High School. This he enjoyed on the whole. Luckily for him he was a tough little boy, rather short for his age but strong. Schools of that day were very rough with plenty of bullying. The fragile, nervous types had a terrible time. Fergus had not been at the

The Quarter, Paris, c. 1906, Manchester City Art Gallery

High School many days when the champion boxer and bully, who 'ran' the school, pushed him roughly, saying, "So you're the new boy. I hope you know your place here." At this, Fergus hit him on the nose, drawing blood. Of course a fight started, but the P.T. instructor happened to be passing and he stopped it, saying, "If you want to fight, do it properly with the gloves on. The best man wins." He arranged for a boxing match between them next night in the gym, when the whole school would attend. Fergus always remembered that fight. It was a foregone conclusion that the cocky new boy hadn't a chance. The handsome school hero, bigger and older, would wipe the floor with him. It turned out the other way. Fergus was wiry, quick on his feet, with a good eye for a punch and for dodging one. He had mixed with a very tough crowd of boys in Leith and knew how to handle the dirty tricks in fighting. There was no knock-out, but the instructor stopped it, declaring Fergus the winner. The school cheered and suddenly he found himself highly popular. To his opponent's credit, he congratulated Fergus and they became friends, forming a partnership to 'run' the school together!

From then on, Fergus enjoyed his life at school. He was quite good at lessons, liked Latin and French and always retained his interest in the derivation of words. The P.T. instructor trained him to box properly and he kept it up till he was about twenty-five. His interest in it was permanent and he would explain to me the finer points of balance, timing etc., but I never developed enthusiasm for watching people hit each other. However, if that is what they want to do, boxing is certainly the best way to do it.

The early days at Leith must have been a struggle, but Fergus's father had a flair for spotting cheap property in places that he could see would go up in value, due to a new road or bus service, and so could be sold at a profit. He must

have gone into some sort of partnership with a builder.
Anyway, gradually things improved and the family moved
to Edinburgh.

All through his life Fergus was devoted to his father and
never tired of talking about him. He told me how, as a small
boy on a bus to school, he met a friend of the family who said,
"And how is that nice old man your father?" Fergus looked
him straight in the eye and said, "My father is the finest man
in the world." No further conversation!

It was Fergus's mother who gave him his first lessons in art. When he was a very small boy she gave him crayons and paper and suggested subjects he could draw. Later she arranged flowers or fruit as still life, and gave, he said, quite sound criticisms. When he was a little older she told him to draw in the garden—the trees, the flowers and the house. This was long before his High School days, but there—in spite of his success as a fighter and at football, and at cricket—he kept on making sketches and watercolours of the boys, or of the garden at home. He remembered vividly lying under a tree, gazing up at the branches with their millions of leaves, and saying to himself—'When I am a man I will paint *every leaf in that tree*!' What a hope, but the determination and integrity behind the thought was characteristic of his approach to art throughout his life.

Though Fergus enjoyed his schooldays, he was never good at getting up. However, there was a bulldog he was devoted to, so his sisters used to open his bedroom door and the dog would rush up and leap onto his bed, licking his face and pulling off the clothes until he got up.

The house in Edinburgh must have been on the outskirts, for it had a big garden at the back, with apple trees and plum trees, vegetables and flowers. Chickens were kept and also pigeons—fantails and tumblers. Fergus adored the pigeons and they must have sensed it, for every day when he came back from school he ran straight through the house into the garden, and the pigeons landed all over him—head, shoulders, arms.

The bulldog met Fergus at the gate where they had mock fights and wrestled on the grass; unfortunately the dog was too devoted to Fergus and attacked anyone who spoke to him in a voice it didn't like. And worse still, motor-cyclists were deadly enemies to be chased—with disastrous results. So eventually it had to be destroyed and Fergus said this was the first real tragedy of his life. The next dog was a pug, never a favourite with Fergus for he couldn't wrestle with it and it was, he said, too full of its own importance. Then a small greyhound arrived on the scene. It was very young and the pug was delighted, started to educate it, boss it and romp in the garden. This happy relationship ended in another tragedy, for the pug. As the greyhound grew the pug could not keep up with it. They were still friends so the pug would

run between the greyhound's legs and look up in bewilderment at his belly. Then the greyhound would leap ahead and leave the pug waddling behind in efforts to keep up. Eventually the poor pug died of a strained heart.

Meanwhile, the greyhound had taken on the job of getting Fergus up in the morning, and he always knew when Fergus was on the way home so would bound to meet him quite a long way from home. As a greyhound is not exactly built for wrestling, Fergus taught him to stand on his hind legs and box—I was told he was quite a good opponent! The greyhound lived to a good old age, because the last story about him was at least fourteen years later. Fergus, having been much impressed by the wonderful free paintings of Morocco by Arthur Melville of the Glasgow School, decided to go and see for himself the effects of intense light and shadow. He told his family he would certainly not write, and had no idea how long he would stay. It was a cold wet night when he did get back to Edinburgh, so he took a fourwheeler cab. The rain was streaming down the windows, and about half a mile from his home he heard a persistent tapping. It was the greyhound leaping again and again at the window. Fergus stopped the cab and took him in.

It seems that the dog had suddenly insisted on being let out, and Fergus's younger sister (the most Celtic) said "Johnny is on his way home!"

After the last war when we were living in Glasgow, Fergus thought of writing his autobiography. He had been asked to do so many times but, as always, he was absorbed in his painting. Nevertheless, from time to time he jotted down some notes, and in 1960 wrote an article for the *Saltire Review*, Vol. 6. No. 21. 1960, called 'Chapter from an Autobiography'. In it he says:

> When I was a small boy, I was standing on the North Inch
> of Perth watching the movement of the water. I looked away

for a moment and saw a very tall dark man 'loping' along towards me—yes, loping is the word for his action. He came directly towards me and said—'Hullo! my little dark-eyed stranger—you'll never stay here—you'll roam!' and passed on, loped away and left me watching the movement of the water.

The movement of water has fascinated me all my life, partly because an uncle who lived in the Highlands pointed out that the appearance of the surface was greatly affected by the fish feeding. He was a famous angler in his district, and had lived by a river all his life and loved it.

Later, in Edinburgh, I took this uncle to one of the first films, called 'A Highland Trout Stream', which I thought would astonish him. As it finished I said to him—'Isn't it wonderful?' My uncle replied—'Not unlike it, John, but a mere idea!' I thought it was just the usual Heilan' refusal to be astonished, but since, I have realised how right he was: it was like asking me to accept a black and white statement of something I had spent my life watching in colour, in all its different aspects . . . but I am getting involved and complicated—yes!

Fergus's father sent him to spend holidays with relations still living in the Highlands and he never tired of talking of the mountains, the waterfalls, the rivers, the birds and animals. A cousin (whose daughter—Elizabeth Fergusson— I am happy to say is still alive and living in Pitlochry) had a sawmill run by water power which was a great delight to Fergus. All he knew about carpentry he learnt as a boy in that sawmill. And how useful that knowledge was to him when he lived in Paris! He made furniture out of packing cases, besides frames for his pictures.

Fergus loved his uncle, and though he only spent a few holidays with him he fully realised how much he owed to him and the hours he spent talking and teaching the rudiments of fishing and shooting. He was a better pupil at shooting, for which he had a good eye, but he did not enjoy killing things and hated carrying back the soft furry or feathered bodies still warm. His love of animals was less sentimental than mine at the same age but also, I think, less logical. He never questioned the necessity to kill for food.

Besides the sawmill where Fergus spent many hours, he would visit a smithy and watch the sparks fly as horses were shod. Again it was the visually dramatic picture that thrilled him, the blazing fire and red-hot irons against a dark background, and lurid light on smith and horse. But he also liked to talk to the smith, who had a fund of wisdom and made such a deep impression on the small boy that sixty years later he would still talk of it and quote actual phrases.

When in the Highlands, Fergus went off alone to explore the country, but he was solemnly warned not to go to a certain part of the woods: a reputed witch lived there and might put the evil eye on him. Fergus listened attentively, then made his way to that very part. He found a tumbledown cottage (a but and ben) and a very old woman sitting in the doorway. 'Betsy the witch' greeted him solemnly and invited him in. Without hesitation he went, knowing instinctively that she was his kind of person. She gave him some brew to drink and he drank it. At once they were friends and she told him wonderful stories of folklore and history. She knew what herbs and plants had magical properties, and the habits of birds and animals. Whenever he could slip away unnoticed he would visit her, despite all stories of her evil influence he knew that she was good for *him*.

The day he was returning to Edinburgh he went up at dawn to say goodbye to Betsy. She was expecting him and said, "I have something for you". He was handed a small pocket compass, with the words, "We shall not meet again; yours will be a good life, and this will guide you". There were tears in her eyes and in his. He treasured that compass and carried it in his pocket for over thirty years. How he came to lose it he had no idea, it must have been shortly before meeting me because when he told me the story, he was still hoping to find it. He never did.

One day, when his uncle had taken him shooting, they were under a big tree and Fergus noticed a small bird near the top of it. A difficult shot. Could he do it, he wondered. Raising his gun he shot the bird and it fell at his feet. Pointing at it, he looked for approval but was amazed to see his uncle's look of horror. "Oh John, John, how could you do it—the bird was singing!" he said.

Highlanders are not averse to killing, but if it's not a battle, there must be a reason for it, an enemy, revenge, or a mercy killing. But to end the life of a bird in the middle of a wonderful song was a dreadful thing to do. Fergus never forgave himself for having been so insensitive. Later in life, he became aware of the fitness of behaviour in different circumstances. For example, in his perpetual war against flies, carriers of disease and dirt, he always carried a fine mosquito net to fix across the windows and a fly swat in his suitcase! A systematic slaughter of all flies inside the window nets would take place, but we did not use fly papers—how could we be happy with insects beside us caught by their wings and dying slowly? Quick death he thought was a deliverance, but when he could have got two flies together at one stroke, because they were making love he would not do it until their wonderful moment was over.

After the High School, which he was sorry to leave, Fergus went to a boarding school called Blair Lodge not far from Edinburgh. This school, he said, was remarkably advanced for that time and had an intelligent, understanding headmaster. Probably Fergus's father mentioned his son's interest in art, because the Head told the boy to do a drawing of the whole Art Room and bring it to him the next day. It was a large studio full of plaster casts, reproductions of old masters, easels for painting, drawing boards and equipment for clay modelling, an impossible subject taken as a whole. But Fergus realised what was expected of him and having chosen a corner to work in, put down all details with great care. Evidently the headmaster was impressed with the drawing, because he told him he could have the key of the studio whenever he wanted it and could spend any free time he liked working there.

This school paid great attention to the health of the boys, who had plenty of swimming and outdoor sports, as well as boxing and fencing. On the scholastic side Fergus got on with most of the masters and did reasonably well in everything that interested him! But in spite of all his boyhood activities, Fergus always found time to sketch. Unfortunately none of the sketchbooks of this period have survived, but I have a watercolour of some boys in the school grounds. Another interest of his that continued throughout his school and

student life was cycling. To begin with he rode an old penny-farthing bicycle. As he grew up, the new type with pneumatic tyres and wheels of equal size were introduced, but the young of the period thought they were terribly 'cissy' and refused to use them until their superiority was proved by the easy winning of races. Fergus watched the first race in Edinburgh and he said it was quite pathetic, the penny-farthings seemed to be left standing. From then on, the young people demanded the new type of bicycle.

As a small boy, Fergus was immensely proud of his first penny-farthing and quite fearless and foolhardy on it. The brakes were inadequate, but on hills he put his feet on the handlebars and raced down, enjoying the speed. On one steep hill he suddenly saw that the road turned sharply at the foot and a stone wall faced him! He tried to turn, but was not in time. It was lucky this time that his feet were on the handlebars, for he shot straight over the wall. Otherwise, he might have broken his legs on it. He landed on his chin on a gravel path and managed to make his way to a nearby farmhouse. The farmer's wife was horrified when she saw a small boy streaming with blood, but she acted promptly and having washed the wound, she got an egg and having removed the yolk took the whole white in her hand and held it over his chin. Soon it formed a protective skin and stopped the bleeding. She said it was a very old remedy, and gave him some hot milk, after which Fergus insisted on walking home wheeling the remains of his battered bicycle. All his life he had a deep scar on his chin.

When he was a little older, Fergus would sometimes be taken sailing with men more than twice his age, and as he soon became a very good 'hand' he was quite in demand. They put into a harbour occasionally, spent the evening in a pub where Fergus was given lemonade and the others got drunk, before taking the last bus home. Their talk was a revelation to Fergus and it widened his whole outlook on life. On one occasion a member of the party wanted to get off the bus on the way home, but as they were in the middle of nowhere the driver refused to stop. Then someone said "Where's Jamie?" "Oh, he's fell'd!" someone replied. He had indeed fallen from the back of the bus, but nobody worried. There would be no traffic till next day.

From childhood Fergus had no doubt that he would be an artist, a painter, but his father worried about how he would earn a living. With this in mind, Fergus had what he thought was a bright idea. He wanted to please his father, so he would take a medical degree and be a doctor in the Navy. He loved the sea and boats, and argued that as serious cases of illness were sent to hospitals, he wouldn't have much to do, but would visit many countries and be able to sketch and paint to his heart's content. This seemed a good idea, but although the first year of medicine went well, the second failed to hold his interest and he made caricatures of his professors instead of learning, so he did not get through the exams!

It must have been a great disappointment for his parents when he decided not to try again, but to do what he really wanted to do—become a painter. Having made his decision, nothing would move him from it. As usual his father was wonderfully understanding, but of course wanted him to go to Art School. To please his father he presented himself there with a portfolio of his work. He would have been accepted, but when he found that he would have to spend two years drawing from the antique, doing lettering etc., and would not work from a model till his third year, he absolutely refused to go near the place again. He said he must teach himself to paint, and he did.

From these early days Fergus carried a small sketch-book in his coat pocket and sketched everything of interest to him. When he started to paint in oils he wanted to familiarise himself with the medium and made a tiny painting box out of a cigar box, to hold two panels of cardboard 5″ × 4″. The lid made a palette on which he put a squeeze of each essential colour; he cut down two oil brushes to fit in, and secured the whole with an elastic band. *Wherever he went*, he carried this little box in his pocket. At any time he could make a sketch, along Princes Street, in the Gardens, by the sea—and that is how he came to feel happy with oil paint. Fergus showed me these boxes, he made two, and I have them still. They are beautifully made, the wood carefully polished—but he never showed me the sketches he made with them! It was only after his death that I discovered a box of sixty small panels. Fergus thought of them as practice sketches, so I hope he is not too annoyed with me for selling them!

It seems appropriate to end a chapter on Fergus's childhood and adolescence with a remark of his own on the subject: "I was born without a language—which perhaps was lucky for me. When I say it was lucky, I mean that I started with a *Gaelic point of view*, in a surrounding of English!"

The two years of medical studies were fruitful in many ways, but as Fergus made friends among the students he was less inclined to go straight home every night to his mother's wonderful dinners. Several nights a week he would cycle back in the early hours, and even the greyhound had difficulty in getting him out of bed in the morning. His parents grew worried as rumours reached them that he went to the Edinburgh Music Hall, reputed to be the haunt of tarts and drunks. They need not have worried for Fergus never did anything that could interfere with his progress as a painter. Actually, the majority of the medical students went regularly to the Music Hall, and many of them became the most distinguished doctors and surgeons.

Fergus always said the Music Hall gave him his first serious training in art and life and he did innumerable sketches of all the stars of the day. In one programme there might be Dan Leno, G. H. Chirgwin (the white-eyed Kaffir), Marie Lloyd, Little Titch, Vesta Tilley, etc. Each performer had to hold the audience completely or they would have been booed off the stage. They had no support from scenery or lighting, which was quite banal and irrelevant—a palace set, or a wood scene front-cloth. What was the secret of their magic?

Besides the performers, the audience provided interesting material to sketch. The women who strolled around in the intervals were all of easy virtue and beautifully made-up. They wore exaggerated fashions in vivid colours, with huge hats gay with ribbons and flowers.

Fergus was always quite clear in his mind on what would help him to be an artist and what would not, and that was all he cared about. He refused to join his student friends on visits to brothels or drinking parties, but of course would go with them to pubs. There he drank beer, although his companions pressed all kinds of drink on him, hoping to see him drunk but always without success. Then one day, when the pub they were in was about to close, they begged him to take them to a club he belonged to where they might get another drink. He refused, saying he wanted to go home and get some sleep. One of the crowd distracted his attention just as the barman was telling them to drink up, and when he turned again to the bar and swallowed the rest of his beer, he knew that something had been put in it. He felt a surge of unusual aggressiveness and as they went out to the street said, "All right, it's a pity to break up the party—I'll take you to the club. I may

In the Sunlight, 1907, Aberdeen Art Gallery

have to wake the porter, but I think you should all get a drink." When they were inside the place, he insisted they have double whiskies and told them to keep very quiet, and be patient if they had to wait a bit. He would go and give the order. Instead, he walked out of the building and went straight home. He said that was the only time he was drunk enough to do such a thing. He regretted he never knew how long his friends waited for their drinks, no one ever mentioned the incident.

One day an old academic artist, friend of Fergus's parents, came to visit. Fergus took him to the upper room he had made into quite a good studio. The old man was greatly interested in the painting he was shown, but insisted that Fergus would get no further as a painter unless he got a studio away from home, so that he could begin to lead a life of his own. Fergus explained how understanding his parents were, that they never asked who he brought to sit for him, or what time he came in at night. But the visitor replied that a good home was the greatest danger to the creative artist because there seemed no good reason and no excuse for leaving it. He pointed out that the human species were the only form of animate life that tried to keep their young with them into adult life. Throughout the animal kingdom the parents encouraged their young to break away, and didn't expect, or wish, to see them again!

Fergus took this advice to heart and started looking in Edinburgh for a large cheap room with plenty of light. Eventually he found an attic with a big window and wonderful view over the Firth of Forth. It was quite a low rent so he took it at once and started distempering the walls a pale grey—later he preferred white, because he said walls soon turned grey anyway. He transferred all his home studio furniture and books. The only extra he thought essential was a sofa, long enough to sleep on if necessary. So he designed

one and had it made to his specifications, well padded over the back and at each end. It came back to Scotland from France after 70 years (I still have it); it must be one of the most travelled sofas, and you will meet it again, later in this narrative.

I quote a note Fergus made about his painting at this time:

When I got my first studio outside the house, I was painting chiefly in water-colour, and sent the results to the Society of Scottish Artists in Edinburgh. At that time Roche was teaching painting in the R.S.A. School. I hadn't met him and was surprised to hear from him that he liked my water-colours very much, and had sold two of them to someone (or rather, on his encouragement someone had bought two). Then he asked me to come to see him at his studio at 2.30, explaining that everybody said they felt in better form for painting after tea—he agreed so had tea as early as possible. This to me, a young and independent painter, was a most friendly and important invitation. I found him there, working on a painting of a charming girl model, obviously attracted by the charm of the girl's beautiful, fresh colour and youth. I didn't say so, but with my point of view the head and background had no *agreement* forms, only some indication of foliage (might be). I stayed too long of course, and when leaving, was still kept by admiring a *remarkably* free sketch (of Valasquez' Infanta), 5 × 9 I think, made in his sketch-box, in the Prado. With his usual sympathy, he said 'Well if you like it so much, I'll lend it to you to copy'. Of course I couldn't express my thanks, took it and made a free copy. I knew the picture in black and white reproduction. Soon after, Willie Peploe, Peploe's brother, was sitting to me and kept saying how much he liked the painting, so I gave it to him.

I have not yet mentioned Fergus's brother Robert, though Fergus played an important part in his development as a boy. He had been a delicate baby, difficult to keep alive, and Fergus thought he was born to the surprise and dismay of his parents. The Highland nurse had said at the birth, "He's just the shakings o' the pook".

When Robert was about seven, Fergus, twelve years older, must have been a medical student; the boy was still very pale and thin, so Fergus took him to the best doctor in Edinburgh for a thorough examination. The doctor pronounced him below par, but with nothing organically wrong and assured Fergus that all he needed was good food, fresh air and graduated exercises—not too much, but not too little—and no coddling. Cold and rain would not hurt him if properly clothed. He should grow up completely fit and strong. And he did, due to Fergus's care of him.

Their father was persuaded to buy a small second-hand yacht Fergus had found so that he could teach his brother to sail. Fergus made him one of the best 'hands' on a boat, always in request for races. But first he was taught to swim. At the baths, Fergus had explained that even if he could not swim and somehow got pushed into the water, there was no need to panic because he was bound to come up to the surface again. If he took a deep breath when his head was out of the water and he kept his mouth shut, he could go down to the bottom and up again indefinitely till somebody pulled him out. Only a few days later, Fergus took Robert to watch some racing on the Firth of Forth. They were standing on the quay between races when Robert must have stepped back and fallen into the water, but he never called out and when Fergus missed him and jumped in to get him, Robert said he'd been down three times! So the lesson had been useful.

As Robert grew stronger, Fergus taught him to box and when he went to school, although small for his age, he could always hold his own. Besides building up his brother physically, Fergus tried to interest him in reading and in the arts. He took him to concerts and exhibitions and lent him books and art magazines. He even got him to start drawing at which it seems he was quite good, though never really interested. But as he grew up, he went further and further from Fergus's point of view. He decided then and stuck to it, that the arts were a waste of time and an excuse for not working. All artists were layabouts, he would be a stock-broker. His father got him into a stockbroker's office where he did so well that they wished to keep him in the firm, but at twenty, he said they could teach him nothing more, and that Scotland and England were dead ends in big business. He would try his luck in South Africa. So he said goodbye to his parents and never saw them again.

When asked what he was going to take up in South Africa, Robert said, "A pick, I expect." And he did, taking the first job offered, down a mine. He worked quite a while there, mostly with Zulus for whom he had great respect, and they for him—he won their admiration by his skill at wrestling, boxing, swimming and sailing boats. At one time he ran a milk farm and delivered the milk himself. I don't know what else he did, but eventually he got to Johannesburg and into a broker's office, and was soon working on his own. A flair for the movements of stocks and shares resulted finally in his being made Chairman of the Johannesburg Stock Exchange.

It is hard to believe that two brothers could be so different in outlook. Fergus continued steadily refusing to send his pictures to the Scottish Academy Exhibitions, or do the things which would have helped his 'career'. It was only when Guthrie became President of the Academy that he changed his attitude to it. Guthrie was one of the leaders of the now famous 'Glasgow School', known in Edinburgh at that time as 'The Wild Men of the West'. The story of how he became President is interesting and little known. An election for next President was due and it was a foregone conclusion that an old painter of Edinburgh would be elected. Someone did propose Guthrie, but no one voted for him so the old man was duly elected. Unfortunately for him, he died a few days later and as no one had objected to Guthrie being nominated, he automatically became President. Of course this had an effect on the Scottish Academy, and the Glasgow School were all accepted, together with Peploe, Hunter and other progressives.

On the subject of the Glasgow School, as opposed to the Academics, Fergus says in his notes:

> ... By painting I mean using oil paint as a medium to express the beauty of light on surfaces. What we used to call in Scotland 'quality of paint'—with solidity and guts!—not drawing a map-like outline and filling in the spaces, with an imitation of the colour of the object, with the paint.
>
> That is the difference between the 'Glasgow School' paintings and academic paintings. I try to describe it as the difference between Harris tweed, composed of all sorts of colours in wool, and any cheap material dyed one flat colour. Even threadbare Harris tweed still has colour, luminosity and durability, and probably looks better when worn—I think so.

By this time, however, Fergus had decided that he would go and settle in Paris, and nothing could shake his decision. He sold all his books and he had quite a valuable collection: art books and magazines including Aubrey Beardsley's *Yellow Book* from the first number. Fergus later regretted he had parted with them all. He also sold the gold watch his father had given him when he was twenty-one, and his studio furniture (except for the sofa which he sent to Paris).

His sailing friends could not understand his decision to go and live in Paris. One of them before parting said, "My God —never feel the spatter of spray on your brow at the first day of the opening cruise!". In his note recording this, Fergus adds a quote from Kipling, "So for one the wet sail arching, through the rainbow round the bow".

PARIS 1905~1914

I open this Part with Fergus's 'Memories of Peploe' published in the *Scottish Art Review*, because it describes his friendship with Peploe in Edinburgh, and their holidays together in Scotland and in France and so links the two periods.

My memories of S. J. Peploe are the memories of our friendship which was wonderful and interesting all the time. Nothing about it was spectacular. It was merely a happy unbroken friendship between two painters who both believed that painting was not just a craft or profession, but a sustained attempt at finding a means of expressing reactions to life in the form demanded by each new experience. This is quite different from arriving at a way of doing a thing and continuing to do it in a tradesmanlike manner. By life we meant everything that happened to us; and, as we were curious about life, we painted all sorts of things—men, women, children, landscape, sea-pieces, flowers, still-life—anything. All I can do about such a friendship is to give a few glimpses of it in the hope that they will reveal something of my old friend.

Peploe was a great admirer of Henry James and had in himself something of the 'restless analyst'. *What Maisie Knew* was one of his favourite books. I remember him saying that Henry James had created one of his characters, a waiter, from a passing glimpse. Perhaps he was interested in this idea because he himself did not create from passing glimpses.

When he made a portrait he had to ponder long over what he was doing. But painting someone you know really well, can also be very difficult. I tried it for years with my father and mother and never kept any of my attempts. There was too much about them that was beyond anything I could put on canvas. My father had brought me up on Robert Burns; my mother had created my first impression of painting and design by telling me the story of the willow-pattern plate I had my porridge in, when I was a very small boy. I can feel her sitting beside me, a very young woman, telling me about the people crossing the bridge and about the birds. Often today, two pigeons fly past my window making the pattern I remember from my porridge plate. Every time I reach to my willow-pattern butter dish, I think of my mother. This is not a glimpse of her; it is something of her that has become part of my life.

Before we met, Peploe and I had both been to Paris—he with Robert Brough and I alone. We were both very much impressed with the Impressionists, whose work we saw in the Salle Caillebotte in the Luxembourg and in Durand Ruel's gallery. Manet and Monet were the painters who fixed our direction—in Peploe's case, Manet especially. He had read George Moore's *Modern Painting* and Zola's *L'Oeuvre*; I had read nothing about painting. At that time hardly anyone in Britain had heard of Cézanne. I was daft about painting and had given up the idea of medicine to devote myself entirely to it. When we met, S.J. and I immediately became friends and I found great stimulation in telling him my ideas about art. We discussed everything. Those were the days of George Moore, Henry James, Meredith, Wilde, Whistler, Arthur Symons and Walter Pater. I remember sitting on the rocks at the extreme north of Islay and reading Walter Pater's essay on Mona Lisa and discussing it with Peploe. At that time I was very interested in French poetry and claimed that without knowing French thoroughly, I could get a great deal out of Gautier's *Emaux et Camées*, merely as a sound composition of words. S.J. did not admit this, and we discussed it often. We

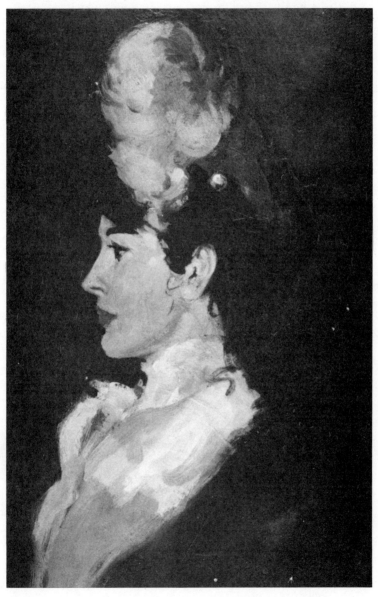

did not know about Druidic incantations, which do not depend for their force on what people call making sense.

Another thing we tried to understand was time, starting from the feeling that while you are doing a thing for the first time, you have done it all before. Then we talked about 'form' in painting and sculpture. In those days what wasn't photographic was called decorative; sculpture meant the Greeks and Michelangelo. I had been much impressed by the bronzes brought back by the Benin expedition and shown in Edinburgh. This exhibition was my introduction to Negro sculpture; I liked it then and still like it.

I tell these things to give an idea of what Peploe and I used to talk about. In the days of our early friendship most of my friends were musicians. We were very much interested in the latest music and its relation to modern painting. S.J. played the piano most sympathetically. I had in my studio one of the first pianos signed by Dettmer. When he came, Peploe always played in with complete understanding of the difference between it and an iron-framed grand. S.J. at the old piano is one of my happiest memories.

On fine days I sometimes called at Peploe's studio in Devon Place. When I asked him to come out, he would say, 'When it's fine outside, it's fine inside!' Most people don't realise how true that is, in a studio planned, decorated and lit for painting. So we sometimes had tea instead of a walk. But we also had long walks and long talks. Often when I had put some idea forward at great length, he would say, 'I'll give you the answer tomorrow.' And he did.

In his painting Peploe always sought to achieve a severe synthesis, to express the character of things with the greatest economy of means. This was also true about his letters. It is easy to believe, as a novelist friend said, that he could have been a very good writer. Once I suggested that he should do something outside painting; he said, 'John, you must remember I'm only a painter.' He didn't mean he was only interested in painting, but that painting was difficult enough for him.

It is strange to think that Peploe started life in a lawyer's office. The lawyer, he said, objected to him spending so much time lying in Princes Street Gardens. So he decided for the Gardens and art. When he announced his decision the lawyer, in the voice and manner of his profession, said, 'Are you sure you have the divine afflatus? You know it is often confused with wind in the stomach.' What was meant by the divine afflatus we can well imagine, knowing the art of that period in the East of Scotland. I think that there can be no doubt about the great contribution Peploe made to Scottish art, not merely by his painting which I think is some of the best ever done in Scotland, but because he became a rallying point for the formation of our group, which carried on the spirit of freedom and colour started by the Glasgow School.

From the start, Peploe and I had been together. When Hunter came back to Scotland from San Francisco after the earthquake, Alex Reid made the three of us and Cadell into a group. We became known in Paris as 'Les Peintres Ecossais'.

John Ressich, the writer, fought very hard for us with great sympathy and intelligence, and entirely disinterestedly—we were very fortunate to have such a courageous friend to help us to hold out till the younger generation came on, this time from the East.

A thing about Peploe that astonished me was that he always thought someone else's painting he had read about must be better than his own. Once when I came back from a visit to the Royal Academy, he asked about the Sargents. I told him that I preferred his own painting. He said, 'That's absurd, there must be something wonderful about those Sargents.'

Once, before I had settled in Paris, Peploe came to join me there. One of his first questions was about the new Salon. When I told him what I thought about it, he said I must be completely underestimating it. I said, 'All right, we'll go.' After wandering through rooms and rooms he said, 'But take me to the good things. I haven't your enthusiasm for walking round galleries.' I said, 'You've seen it all; you've been right through.' It must have been Peploe's respect for official institutions that made him persist in sending work to the R.S.A. where he was generally rejected.

One year we went together to Islay. In others it was to Etaples, Paris-Plage, Dunkirk, Berneval, Dieppe, Etretat and Le Tréport—all happy painting holidays. We worked all day, drawing and painting everything. And we thoroughly enjoyed the food and wine. We agreed on the importance of good food and drink, not fantastic food, but good peasant food in France and good Scots food in Scotland—what's better than good steaks and good Burgundy, good beef and good beer? We enjoyed and took time over our meals—time to eat and talk and draw the things on the table. S.J. loved a book about food I had lent him, *Cakes and Ale,* by Nathaniel Gubbins, (how he would have loved that wonderful book, *The Scots Kitchen,* by Marian McNeill). We got a taste for French food and wine and we found a different way of living. We were always glad to get back to it.

I remember when we arrived at Dunkirk I laughed at the

lightness of the railway carriages. S.J. said, 'What's the matter with them—aren't they adequate?' That was characteristic of him. In his painting, and in everything, he tried to make things adequate; to find the essentials by persistent trial. He worked all the time from nature but never imitated it. He often took a long time to make contact with a place, and was discouraged by failure. He wanted to be sure before he started and seemed to believe that you could be sure. I don't think he wanted to have a struggle on the canvas—he wanted to be sure of a thing and do it. That gave his painting something.

After the last of our early painting holidays in France, S.J. went back to Scotland and I went to Paris and settled there. Of course we wrote to each other a great deal. I wrote long letters trying to explain modern painting. Something new had started and I was very much intrigued. But there was no language for it that made sense in Edinburgh or London—an expression like 'the logic of line' meant something in Paris that it couldn't mean in Edinburgh. I find today that most painters don't understand what happened in Paris before 1914—though hundreds of books have been written about it. This was why I was so glad when, after a few years, Peploe came to live in Paris with Margaret, his charming, sympathetic wife.

By this time I was settled in the movement. I had become a *Sociétaire* of the Salon d'Automne and felt at home. Peploe and I went everywhere together. I took him to see Picasso and he was very much impressed. We went to the Salon d'Automne where we met Bourdelle, Friesz, Pascin and others. He started to send to the Salon d'Automne. I was very happy, for I felt that at last he was in a suitable milieu, something more sympathetic than the R.S.A. He was working hard, and changed from blacks and greys to colour and design. We were together again, seeing things together instead of writing about them.

Things I really like—perhaps I should say love—often make me want to laugh. One day Peploe and I went to see the Pelliot Collection. As we wandered through it we were

suddenly halted, fixed by an intensity like a ray, in front of a
marble head of a Buddha, white marble, perhaps, with a
crown of beads painted cerulean blue. I can't remember
anything in art with a greater intensity of spiritual feeling.
We both stood for what seemed a long time, just looking.
Then I laughed. I apologised to S.J. for breaking the spell.
With his usual understanding he said, 'At a certain point
you've either to laugh or cry.'

This was the life I had always wanted and often talked
about. We were a very happy group: Anne Rice, Jo
Davidson, Harry and Bill McColl, Yvonne and Louis de
Kerstratt, Roffy the poet, La Torrie, mathematician and
aviator. Other good friends in the Quarter were E. A. Taylor
and Jessie King, who made a link with the Glasgow School.

We used to meet round the corner table at Boudet's restaurant. We were mothered by the waitress, Augustine, a wonderful young woman from the Côte-d'Or, very good-looking with calm, live, dark eyes and crisp, curly, black hair —very strong and well made, a character as generous as the finest Burgundy; a perfect type of that great woman, the French *paysanne*. When you came in far too late, tired and empty, Augustine would go across to the butcher and demand through the bars, a *bon chateaubriand à quatre-vingt-dix*, cook it perfectly herself and present it to you as if you had a perfect right to be an artist. This with such grace that you did not feel in the least indebted. Looking back, we realise it is not possible for us to express our indebtedness; what we can do is to say that every picture we painted at that period is partly Augustine. Her health, in the best burgundy! God bless her. Then there was Madame Boudet at the pay desk, sonsie and easy to look at—and very understanding. When we couldn't pay we did our signed and dated portraits on the back of the bill. After dinner we went to L'Avenue for coffee and music. La Rotonde was then a 'zinc' with seats for three only.

It was in these pre-war days that Middleton Murry and Michael Sadler came over and asked me to be the art editor of *Rhythm*. Peploe contributed to it. Later Murry came with Katherine Mansfield. We were all very excited with the Russian Ballet when it came to Paris. Bakst was a *Sociétaire* of the Salon d'Automne and used all the ideas of modern painting for his *décor*. Diagilev made a triumph, surely even greater than he had hoped for. No wonder S.J. said these were some of the greatest nights of his life. They were the greatest nights in anyone's life—*Sheherazade*, *Petruchka*, *Sacre du Printemps*, Nijinski, Karsavina, Fokine. But we didn't spend all our evenings at the Russian ballet; there was the Cirque Médrano, the Concert-Mayol and the Gaité-Montparnasse.

This was our life in Paris till the *Grand Prix*. Then, where should we go for the summer? One year we went to Royan

where Bill, Peploe's elder son was born. Another year we went to Brittany. But I had grown tired of the North of France; I wanted more sun, more colour; I wanted to go south to Cassis. I told S.J., but he didn't think it was a good idea—too hot for young Bill. I was sorry, but decided to go without him. One day in the Boulevard Raspail, S.J. saw on the pavement just near his door, a paper with the word 'Cassis' on it. He decided to take the risk. We arrived to find it quite cool and Bill didn't suffer at all. We had his birthday party there and, after a lot of consideration, chose a bottle of Château Lafitte instead of champagne. Château Lafitte to me now means that happy lunch on the verandah overlooking Cassis bay sparkling in the sunshine.

My studio in Paris was being pulled down so I decided to stay in the south somewhere on the coast between Cassis and Nice. I took a house and settled in Cap d'Antibes. The

Rhythm, 1911, The University of Stirling

Peploes went back to Scotland and, very soon, the 1914 war drove me back to London. After that we saw much less of each other. But whenever I came to Scotland to see my mother, the next person to see was S.J. We resumed our walks in Princes St. as though the break had been hours instead of years. We laughed a great deal and got a lot of fun out of everything. One summer afternoon we went to the Zoo and laughed with the seals, but were suddenly checked when an eagle looked at us as though we were mud. We were depressed to see the elephant in his loose box. That's how it was with us. We enjoyed simple things—a good meal, a good picture, the light on a cloud.

As I think about Peploe, I remember a day when we were painting in a wood near Paris-Plage. The light on the tree trunks set me wondering. What paint should I use to express it? When Peploe came up we agreed that it needed something like pastel. That was the beginning of our awareness that oily paint is not for everything. There were many beginnings like that which each of us, in his own way, developed in his painting. Our friendship and our shared experiences are like the willow-pattern plate that brings my mother back to me. When things are really important, it becomes impossible to express them except by some extraordinary release over which we have no control.

I am writing too much—just as though I were talking to Peploe; but it is difficult to be brief about a wonderful friendship that lasted a lifetime. It was, I think, one of the best friendships that has ever been between two painters.

Fergus first visited Paris in 1897. He stayed in the Haute Loire Hotel, and in his note book says: it was advertised in the splendid little magazine *Le Quartier Latin*—to which I am tremendously indebted.

This hotel is where Boulevard Raspail crosses Boulevard Montparnasse. It was the cheapest he could find, but clean and, as in all French hotels, with good beds.

I quote again some passages from 'Chapter from an Autobiography' which relate to this visit:

I saw the Impressionists in the Salle Caillebotte, Manet, Renoir, Monet and the rest. In the Caillebotte Gallery (really a shed) there were large open ventilators under the picture line, showing the light on the leaves in the garden and letting in the sunshine and air—harmonizing very well with the pictures. I suppose it was not intended to be a real gallery like the Luxembourg—but they'd got these things and had to house them, so! . . .

I painted in the Luxembourg Gardens, on the quais, and barges. I knew boats, I liked the open air and the idea of being in an art school didn't suit me at all. I was attuned to the movement of water and light on water. . . .

The creamery where I ate had good pictures on the wall. Then there were the Independents: the first show of theirs I saw was on one of the quais and I had to walk on duck-boards because the river rose too much. There I saw new points of view in painting—for example an Odilon Redon with animals in the sky.

I went everywhere I thought there might be a gallery or a dealer, and I decided that as I had no money I should dress accordingly. I wore a blue jersey and the blue suit I used to wear for sailing, grey with salt water. I must have looked a tramp, but I didn't want the dealers to get the impression that I might be a buyer. A portrait painter, MacCameron, became a great friend. He was very well dressed and we must have looked a strange couple. He was very practical and successful—a very sympathetic chap.

My only contact with art schools was at the Colarossi. A model sat there every afternoon and there was no teacher; you paid each time you went. There I met an Englishman who took me to the creamery we called 'The Hole in the Wall', just below the Hotel de la Haute Loire. It was very good food, but the great thing was the group. Bringing me to 'The Hole in the Wall' changed Paris for me—from being entirely alone, to being with a wonderful group of young artists, mostly with bursaries from different countries. Frazer, for example, most successful sculptor student; MacMonnies came sometimes; Myron Barlow, a new name as a guide to the period, probably 1895, when I was twenty-one. We had early lunch and late dinner and between meals painted or went round the galleries.

In summer the weather was beautiful and I went out to the country: Giverny or Montigny, to see in nature what I saw in the Impressionists' paintings of it. I came back to dinner at the creamery. One day I was presented to a new man. I had a strap over my shoulder, with heavy wooden tin-lined paint box filled with paints, with oil and turpentine in bottles and an easel. The man I was presented to said, 'You're an artist,' looking at my paintbox. I said, 'Not yet, but I hope to be.' He asked if I had been in the country all day and I said, 'Yes—marvellous!' 'But aren't you tired carrying that heavy box?' he asked. That was one of the most helpful things said to me. I have never since carried a heavy box of paints . . . but I have made any number of sketches and notes.

In 1905, when Fergus started his journey to settle in Paris, he must have been very tired, with sorting, packing and final arrangements. He went by Dieppe because it was cheapest, and sat on deck in a thick, long overcoat, his kitbag beside him. It was wet and rough. He was a good sailor, but he had had no rest and when he finally got on the train for Paris, he must have been completely exhausted, for I found this note:

> In the train from Dieppe to Paris I sleep on the bosom of a Frenchman's wife, to the great amusement of the carriage.

In his notes he continues:

> I was alone in Paris. I should have said long ago how indebted I have always been to the Studio magazine—evident in the fact that I went to Paris with a very good article about me in the magazine. But more than that—Henri Frantz was writing in Paris for the Studio at the time, and I had an introduction to him from the wonderfully sympathetic Editor. All of us are indebted to him, though the young ones don't know it.
>
> Frantz was immediately helpful with excellent advice. For some years I had been sending to the Salon, where Jacques Blanche and the other good men had hung me advantageously. Frantz said, "Yes, but the place you should send to is the Salon d'Automne".
>
> Strange how a few really sympathetic words of advice can count. I took Frantz's advice and they gave me a wall to myself—and a few years later made me a Sociétaire. To me, considering myself a revolutionary, this was a very great honour—and being based on the Glasgow School, it had the effect of confirming my feeling of independence, the greatest thing in the world, not merely in art but in everything. I'll die fighting for it.
>
> It has been said on reaching the border of France, 'Ici commence la Liberté'. I agree. Vive la France. Let's not forget, ever, the Auld Alliance.

Well, I was in Paris, without money or rich relations to call on, often realising it was quite stupid, but repeatedly encouraged by what someone has called 'le bon air de Paris, qui semble contenir les effleuves amoureuses et les emanations intellectuelles'! It seemed to change my point of view, and one may say that the advice of Henri Frantz was what carried me through—for I had been accepted by the people I had most respect for. As an artist nothing could be more important.

On the other side of the river there were the Galleries and the dealers' galleries—Durand Ruel, with the most sympathetic people in charge, willing to discuss painting with *me*, a young unknown painter; the Salle Caillebotte, most helpful: Parnassus right enough, but *not trying* to be. An artist was an important part of life and could be *fichu pour quatre sous*, yet be, not the *Grande Condé*, but an important

person if he could paint or had ideas. The grocer would
listen to his ideas . . .

Fergus told me how Peploe then joined him on a short
visit and how they sat on a bench in the Boulevard Edgar
Quinet, facing the cemetery, and discussed for hours whether
Fergus should take a studio at a yearly rent of £12.
Eventually, Fergus decided to risk it! I quote again:

> So here I was in Montparnasse by chance, but uncon-
> sciously accepting the name, as all in order—perhaps because
> I had been so long accustomed to the name by Robert Burns.
> Unlike Passy, there was no disappointment for me in
> Montparnasse. I can look back to nothing but happiness.
> Difficulties, yes!
>
> My studio at 18 Bd. Edgar Quinet, was comfortable,
> modern and healthy. My concierge most sympathetic. Life
> was as it should be and I was very happy. The Dôme, so to
> speak, round the corner; L'Avenue quite near; the 'Concert
> Ronge' not far away—I was very much interested in music;
> the Luxembourg Gardens to sketch in; Colarossi's class if I
> wanted to work from the model. In short, everything a
> young painter could want.

At this period, Fergus was making sketches in cafés all the
time—I have dozens of sketch books with hundreds of
wonderful sketches! Some of them he enlarged and did in
charcoal or ink, sometimes with touches of colour. He
mounted them, then took them to dealers—I am sure this
is the only time in his life he did such a thing, but they were
easy to sell and enabled him to settle to serious painting.

About this time, on a holiday with Peploe at Paris-Plage,
Fergus met a most attractive American girl, whom he found
was also very intelligent—an unusual combination which
appealed to him greatly. She was already a successful book

illustrator, but at her art school she had been told that she would never become a painter in oils. She was coming to Paris to do sketches of the top dressmakers' spring collections. Fergus said she must start painting in oils, and that he would make her a first class painter which he did. She rented a studio and for eight years lived and worked in Paris. Her pictures were well hung in big Paris exhibitions and often sold. Later she had success in America and London.

On one of Fergus's early visits to Paris-Plage with Peploe, they were staying at a charming bourgeois hotel and had noticed a large family that filled one table. Because the mother, a plump, good-looking woman, and her children wore clothes of beautiful colours, Fergus said, "The woman sailed into the dining-room with a bunch of children in each hand like bouquets of flowers".

One day Fergus was on the beach looking for subjects and saw this woman sitting alone knitting. At once he started a sketch of her. Before long she rolled up her wool, but as she turned to put the knitting in her bag she noticed Fergus drawing and said, "Are you making a sketch? I can stay a little longer if you like". Of course Fergus was delighted and thanked her warmly. As they walked back to the hotel she said, "I understand how important these sketches can be, my husband is an artist. I am Madame Renoir".

John Wanamaker, a great American retailer and patron of the arts, must have been impressed by Fergus's pictures in the Autumn Salon, for he got a letter asking him to call to discuss a proposition. Wanamaker said how much he liked Fergus's painting and that he had a trade magazine he would like him to edit on the artistic side, doing headings for articles and tail-pieces, and also designing posters. This seemed a good idea as Fergus would draw a regular salary every six months, and the work should not take too much of his time.

Wanamaker asked what guarantee Fergus could give him for the salary he would receive in advance. Fergus replied, "Well, take a good look at me. With your experience of judging character you should know if I will keep my side of the bargain". Wanamaker smiled and said, "I just wondered what you would say. Go to the office and draw your first six months salary". This was a great lift financially and enabled Fergus to buy good paints and canvases that he could not afford before. Many of his early pictures are painted on strawboard.

He quite enjoyed designing paper headings and doing posters. But there was always a deadline for posting to New York and of course Fergus was always late. He usually had to get a cab to the station and post his parcel on the train. One day, being later than usual, he couldn't find a cab. The cabbies were all at their evening meal. He knocked at the shelter where they ate, but all the men refused. Fergus offered to pay double fare, but they still shook their heads and one of them shouted—"Mais monsieur, il faut manger!" In France, nothing must interfere with eating.

I fear Fergus missed the post on that occasion. And eventually he found he was spending far too much time on designing for Wanamaker, because everything he did had to be the best he could do. So he gave it up at the end of the year for which he had contracted. I think one of the last posters he did was of Blériot's first flight across the Channel. The plane had left at dawn, July 25th, 1909, in a high wind and with no modern publicity. Fergus made sketches of it as it came over and landed in England.

When Fergus met Jo Davidson, the American sculptor whose work is now very well known, he was still very hard up. A Russian Jew, he had been born in New York, where his mother kept the family by making neckties and Jo, as a boy, sold newspapers. I don't know how he got to Paris, but he did, and was then doing modelling in some kind of shed. He took Fergus to see it and Fergus was much impressed by the work; but Jo said no one wanted to buy works by unknown sculptors. Fergus said, "If you must make money to live, why not do portrait busts?" "I've never done any portraits," said Jo. "Then why not try?" and Fergus took up some clay and modelled a small head of himself (which I still have); then he told Jo to do a head of him, and he did. From that moment he never looked back, though for several years the going was tough.

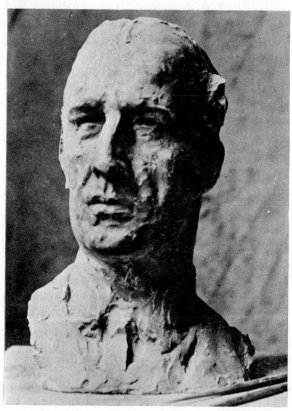

Jo and Fergus became the greatest of friends, though their characters and outlooks on life were very different. Fergus got worried, being a canny Scot, that when Jo did make a good sale, he would gather his friends together and take them for a night out in Montmrtre and blow the lot! When he remonstrated, pointing out that Jo could have lived for a month on what he spent in one night, Jo said, "But Johnnie, you don't understand, because you had a good youth: I sold papers, barefooted in wet and snow in New York". This was true and Fergus said no more.

Though always serious about his work, Jo loved parties and took every chance to go out and meet people. Eventually he met a very beautiful and elegant woman, Yvonne de Castrat, who had a maison de haute couture off the Champs Elysées. She sat to him and they eventually got married. It was a most successful partnership as Yvonne had the entry into a social world which Jo enjoyed. Many commissions followed, eventually more than he could cope with, so he kept raising his prices! Andrew Mellon, one of the richest men in America, commissioned Jo to do a bust of him. At the last sitting he said, "Well, what do I owe you?" When Jo named a very big figure, Mellon protested and Jo said, "But haven't you got it?" Mellon laughed and said, "You win," and wrote a cheque for the full amount. They remained good friends.

I don't know when Jo went back to the States, but he did many busts there, including President Roosevelt, with whom he became very friendly. I'm sure it is no exaggeration to say that he 'busted' everyone of note in the social, political, scientific and artistic worlds of his period. Of all the notable people who sat to him, he told us that the two whom he would always remember as the most interesting to talk to were Einstein and Charles Chaplin.

More from Fergus's notes:

At the top of Bd. Montparnasse, in the direction of Bd. St. Michel and opposite the Bal Bullier, was a charming café, la Closerie des Lilas. It had a very large terrace and seats under the trees where, later, Paul Fort (King of the Poets) held open meetings on Thursdays, for all the poets. When a monarch, meeting this most distinguished poet for the first

time, said 'But how is it we have never met?' The reply was, 'Parceque nous sommes venus par des differentes routes— moi, par la route des poetes, vous par la route des rois.' You see what that means . . .

Further down the Boul Miche was the wonderful Café d'Harcourt, where they had a lively Hungarian band that used a metal tray with knives and forks and spoons on it, to reinforce, very successfully, their music. But for me the great attraction was the girl frequenters. They were chiefly girls employed by dressmakers and milliners and wore things they were working at, mostly too extreme from a practical point of view, but with that touch of daring that made them very helpful—they were a great help to me.

I made what was considered a very bad break, by taking a perfectly respectable girl artist to this café—the café was not concerned about respectability—L'Avenue was where you took respectable girls, but my girl friend survived it. We always came down to the d'Harcourt after dinner to make sketches of these charming girls, who were quite pleased to be drawn and didn't become self-conscious or take frozen poses. Well, one night my artist friend and I sat beside a very good-looking lad with a nice girl—they were apparently and quite rightly pleased with each other. We were sketching people round while they were beside us, so neither looked at them nor heard what they were saying, but I remembered the lad vaguely and with sympathy.

In my studio in Paris, not the original one by this time, I had to arrange some way of having my morning bath at the front door. I had floor space of about four feet square beside the wash-basin and I had covered with solid linoleum up to about a foot high, quite watertight. I did the putty part myself to make sure, so, with a rubber bath I always carry with me —even going to the highlands of Scotland—and a basin, I could splash as much as I liked. Often I had to open the front door, slightly, if I was in the nude, to explain to callers. When Epstein wanted to do something about the Wilde monument, for example.

Well, one of these times I looked out to find a couple of young men. They wanted 'to talk about things', I told them to come back later and I'd be very pleased. They did and introduced themselves as Middleton Murry and Michael Sadler. At once I got the feeling that I had seen one of them before. It took some time, but presently I got it—one was the lad I'd seen at the d'Harcourt with the girl: he was Middleton Murry who was to become a great friend. A lad I admired for his honesty and artistic intelligence.

They had come, they said, because they had seen my picture in the Autumn Salon called 'Rhythm'. They had decided to start a magazine and wanted to call it Rhythm and use my picture as a cover. Of course I said I'd do anything I could to help them, but I didn't think Rhythm was a good title—it was (at that time) a word hardly ever used and to most people meant nothing. Some such word as 'Quest' would be better, I suggested. But no, they wanted Rhythm, so I was immediately with them solidly and agreed to become Art Editor. I adapted my picture to make a cover. My only condition was that it would be cheap, not a de luxe magazine. I wanted any herd boy to be able to have the latest information about modern painting from Paris, which was then undoubtedly the centre of modern painting. They agreed and Rhythm duly appeared at 1/-, well printed and presented. From all accounts it was a success.

One of Fergus's best friends, Harry McColl, a business man working in Paris, took him to the races at Chantilly, and to a smart café afterwards where he might make sketches. Suddenly he saw a tall and beautiful woman in a pink dress, standing by a table talking to friends. He quickly made a rough sketch, with notes on the colours. He said to Harry, 'That is a most beautiful woman, I must do a picture from this sketch.' He did, and sent it to the Autumn Salon where it was well hung. On the opening day, Fergus saw a tall, handsome young man standing in front of the picture. The

Rose Rhythm: Kathleen Dillon, 1916, Mrs. K. Morrison

young man turned, saying "Are you Fergusson? I've just bought your picture—that is my wife."

Fergus was delighted and they talked. It turned out that the young man was the son of the President of the Argentine! He begged Fergus to return with him and do more paintings of his wife. He would buy anything Fergus painted for him and, of course, pay all his expenses. When his friends saw Fergus's paintings of his wife they would all want their wives painted by him, and he would make a great deal of money in a very short time. But Fergus realised that the wives could not all be as good looking as the President's daughter-in-law, and he could not refuse to paint them on that account! Also, the social life inevitably involved in staying with the President's son was not for him. So regretfully, he refused. Of course his friends thought he was mad. . . .

I have already told how I came to meet Fergus and how helpful he was when I came to Paris. Here is the first letter I had from him:

Dear Miss Morris,
 Four of the people I invited turned up and enjoyed your dancing very much. Another sent friends, so that's always something.
 I wish you'd let me know how long you're going to stay. I'm trying to arrange for you to come to the studio of a woman I know—she was there yesterday. She is an artist and has a big studio. She knows everybody. Let me know if you will come and dance, at tea time I suppose. If you say so I'll ask her. I think this as good as you can do, or as I can do for you, so let me know at once if you can.
 She is unfortunately going to Poland soon, so I must ask you to let me know at once. Next Wednesday is her last At Home. Come if you can dance, for although I can't

promise any help—I'm no good at this 'boosting business'—
I certainly won't waste your time intentionally, or through
carelessness.

I hope you're fit. Best wishes,

J. D. Fergusson

Of course I went and danced at Madame Mutermilch's
studio, and she at once offered me the loan of it while she was
in Poland! I joyfully accepted it.

This was the beginning of a new life for me. I had never
lived completely alone, on my own, before. The first few
nights I hardly slept; the studio was so big and high, and
part of a very old building, so there were many strange
noises and I felt quite cut off from any human communica-
tion. But after a few days I got to love the feeling of isolation
and the freedom it gave, and I was very sad to leave it. In this
studio I could practice my own dancing, instead of teaching
others all day. I also started trying to paint in oils.

Fergus was very preoccupied with his own painting, but
he was at the Café du Dôme most evenings, and there I met
de Segonzac, Friez, Vlaminck and Digremont, who designed
for the theatre and was an enthusiast on Scottish things—he
had a collection of bagpipes and kilts.

One day Fergus took me to Gertrude Stein's Salon. She
was very friendly and asked us to come again, but Fergus
said to me later that he did not want to be launched as one
of her discoveries, so we never returned. She was certainly
responsible for getting Picasso the recognition he deserved.

There was a little Russian woman artist, I think called
Vaselief, who opened her studio twice a week to artists. She
made a large cauldron of peasant soup. One paid a small sum
on entering and was served with a generous bowl of it, and a
chunk of bread—no extra charge for a second helping.
Conversations and arguments flourished, though no drink
was available. I enjoyed these evenings very much.

When I left Paris in due course, Fergus had already decided he would look for a small house on the Riviera and settle there. Frank Harris, whom he had always liked and defended saying he was a modern Robin Hood because he exploited the rich to help the artists offered Fergus his flat in Nice, so that he could explore the whole coast from there. This, Fergus gratefully accepted. He cycled to Ventimiglia and from there to Marseilles and back keeping to the coast road. He decided without hesitation that the Cap d'Antibes was the ideal spot. The Romans had come to the same conclusion. In 1913 this coast was deserted in the summer as the casinos were all closed.

Fergus found a tiny house on the Cap. It was off the Avenue de la Salis, built for a gardener's cottage behind a modest villa suitably named 'La Farandole', one of the traditional dances of France. The little house was new and clean, but except for a fig tree and a small vine the ground was quite bare. Fergus had hoped to find a house with a garden, but when the agent told him to go ahead and make one, he remembered how long that job took in Scotland and felt doubtful. However he took the house and was soon amazed to discover how fast everything grows on the Riviera, and how easy it is to make a garden there. Soon, I had this letter from him—

17th September, 1913.
My dear flapper, I've just come back from the hut. Cycled there and back, a beautiful night. The sea was really wonderful and the hut isn't at all bad, I can make something of it. If you don't come down, you're a rotter and no sport and everything else that's bourgeois. As to your reputation— hell! Come down 'on the flap'. Come disguised? I mean physically, as a flapper. No one will notice you, there are hundreds of them here, just the same, better I mean; besides, I'll give you a chance to 'live the part'. No, come just as the

natural girl. That'll be charming. Anyway you mustn't imagine this is a chic place like Nice or Cannes, I've seen no English or chic people here at all, that's why I took the place. The villas near are let only in the summer apparently. If you lose this dam'd reputation we'll make another for you and a better one. I feel like lasting some time yet with the sun and sea air and soforth—and I may be able to do something. So come on. I'll promise to hang only landscapes on the walls, or flowers. If you like I'll send home for my boxing gloves, my pipes, my golf-clubs, and we'll hang the gloves and the fencing foils above the mantelpiece in the top room, I've a fireplace there. Cheer-oh and I'll have my hair curled at the sides and stick out my chin and we'll play at being the Gibson boy and girl and I'll forget I'm nearer 50 than 18. There's a golf course near, so there you are.

At nights we'll sit before the fire or play bridge, or talk golf. I'll sleep on the sofa. There's a key to your room, so the whole thing's in order. By the way, do you tango yet? Perhaps that's not the right sort of question to ask. Too Parisian. Pardon.

Well Meg—seems to me worthwhile, but I don't know what you're thinking about. Perhaps if he's very nice and has money and will marry you and all that sort of thing, you'd better give this a miss, but write as soon as you decide not to come, for there are things I needn't bother about immediately in that case. Give news in your letter—but of course you'll be too busy. Well a postcard then.

Yours JDF

Of course I was determined to join Fergus at Antibes, sometime, somehow, but at that moment it was out of the question. I had several engagements to fulfil with my troupe, and was preparing the first printed prospectus of the school. I had quite an impressive list of patrons, including Ellen Terry and Gordon Craig. I asked Fergus if I might add his name— then another letter arrived:

7th October, 1913. Nice.

Dear Meg,

. . . the School seems to me to be a very good idea . . .
certainly, put my name down and I'll try to get people
interested as I did for Rhythm . . . I can quite understand
that drawing, letter-writing etc., is not in your line. I'm
anxious to see your new photos. Hope they're good.

Now! as folk would say—look here! Listen! I've taken a
little villa at Antibes, 40 minutes from here in the train. I went
over the coast as far as Italy and this is the best there is for
the money. The villa is very small but only a year old, and
therefore absolutely clean. On the ground floor there's a very
nice little kitchen and a decent room; on the first floor, a very
good room and a good bedroom, faces the sun all day. Small
garden which I'll make quite good. It's away from the town
about 15 minutes, 5 minutes from the electric train, 20
minutes from the station—on the road to nowhere, therefore
no cars passing. Three other villas near, that's all. The sea at
the bottom of the road, about 100 yards away; it looks across
to Nice and on to Italy, Leghorn and Florence, about 200
miles distant. There's a little port for boats; a road round, with
rocks and pine trees and 10 minutes away on the other side,
a fine sand beach with pine trees. It is practically an island
and quite quiet. Don't need to dress at all—I mean dress up.

The room upstairs has a balcony and is quite nice, not
overlooked at all so one can go about there nude. The top flat
can be kept private—I don't intend to let people up—and it
is of course shut off and the staircase is narrow. So there you
are, what more do you want? You can walk round the
island; go to the town which is very interesting; bathe off the
rocks or on the sand beach; lie among the pine trees and
watch the sea—looking over at Nice, Menton, with the Alps
behind; sit in the sun in the garden; go to Nice or Cannes
and see chic people. I hope to have a boat; I'll lend you my
bicycle which I've just got new tyres for and spent two days
putting into first class shape—bring your bloomers; go and
blow in your money at Monte Carlo; go to the Opera there,

or concerts; walk to dozens of places or take the air; go up mountains . . . really, what more do you want? There's plenty fruit of course. The place, I mean the town, is a tremendously clean place. The drinking water is said to be perfect—no danger of typhoid or anything of that sort. Well hell, what do you want? Ostrich feathers? There's an ostrich farm near Nice. Then, if it's not blazing sun, it's exceptional, and the air is either off the sea, or the snow-clad Alps. All around my place are flower nurseries, fields of flowers. No slums. Well I suppose you'll say it would be all right with a man, instead of an artist, a bloody artist . . .

My furniture is on the way I expect, and in a fortnight I should be installed. I'm feeling very fit, too fit, so I hope to do a decent imitation of a man for you . . .

Really Meg, apart from all joking, this place is wonderful. I don't see what more one could want and as I walk along the promenade in the evening I wish you were with me to share it. I thought of you tonight—I went into the town, to the port, at twilight. It was wonderful. Thought of these nights in the Champs Elysées. Really, since we both can really walk and enjoy going about, this place is for us. I'm very fit—you know, when you feel spring in your leg muscles.

Well here I am, down here, absolutely free. I haven't spoken to anyone—that is, talked to anyone for a month and am glad of it; but I would like to have a housewarming and start down here altogether—and as you're the only woman I'm interested in, I'd like it to be with you. I'm sorry I can't help on the money side, but I can't. I need it all, as I have no credit down here. Don't know a soul and have no chance of making money that's out of the question. But if you can at all come down, it would really give you a new point of view on things. Altogether it's different and much better. If you can, try to arrange for three weeks at least. Let me know. About the 26th I'll be ready to receive you (bar accidents) in every sense. So make an effort. Buck up and come down.

Best wishes, yours JDF

I'm sending your drawings. If anyone happens to ask where

I am, say I've taken a place on the Riviera—NO. I don't want to see anyone.

Of course this letter made me quite desperate to go to Antibes, but I couldn't possibly get away till the Christmas holidays when the School would be closed. Even this was not going to be easy to arrange, as in that very unpermissive age it wasn't surprising that my mother and my aunt who between them did all the secretarial side of the School knew that any breath of scandal would stop most parents sending their children to me. It was not long since we had moved to our Chelsea premises at a rent of £100 a year, double what we had paid in Endell Street, and we were also moving to another flat in King's Road. What I said to Fergus about all this I do not know, but shortly I received the following from him—

October 15th, 1913. Nice.
Dear Meg you silly ass? your letter really is quite wonderful, you know what I mean? And as to the photos—the peacock one reminds me of Paris and that reminds me that I've just been going over my address book rubbing out addresses and I came across—Mrs. Robson, 1 Place Wagram, Paris—she might help you a great deal with the School. She knows all the smart people, goes everywhere, Paris and London. Don't forget about her, she could even help you in America I believe. I like her very much and I don't think she hates me.
    Well—the photos. Isn't the peacock one rather, um! er 'riskie' what? They're for the most part thin. I know they're proofs, it's not that: they're anaemic. But no doubt you know your own affairs. You look very well in them all; in the peacock one you look fatter than when in Paris. In it, your skin is the same tone as the background and, therefore, disappears, which, as the late Mr. Euclid would say, is absurd. The same is true about the white skirt in the others. Of course I could explain it much better if we were together—I mean

with a chaperone of course. To start with, such photos are no good for reproduction—except on the very best paper and <u>handled</u> by a careful engraver. On anything but first class paper they will simply disappear and the engraver will supply something in their place.

Isn't business a tiresome thing? I've been spending my mornings going over my letters and writing business letters. Are those stockings in the photos the 'darn no more' hole-proof sort? Where do you get them? My socks are in a frightful state. Can you get mens? I mean strong woollen in what they call clerical grey—I always wear that colour.

The last photo is the one of you standing with your hands on your hips. Are they taken by the man you told me about? The white-against-white man, I mean. Well, <u>perhaps</u> they'll be better when they're finished, as the people say about my pictures. By the way, how do you come to have expensive underclothing? I thought you were hard up. Answer these questions will you?

Then about your letter. You ask me to answer questions too—well, there's no need to. If there's going to be the slightest chance of doing you harm (coming here), there's nothing more to be said. Of course, not being a woman, I never think about what people think. I never did on my own account: if I had I would be worth lots of money by now and would have asked you out in my stinko car instead of asking you to walk.

I no more know how long I'm going to stay here, than how long I'm going to like you. I refuse to stay with anyone, anything, or in any place if I don't like to. I'm free, or as nearly so as one can be. I am down here where I don't know anyone and am dam'd glad to be. Their affairs don't interest me.

If you had come down, you'd probably have found that I was the one to lose interest first in the matter of sexualising. I'm dam'd sorry to say so, but I can't keep it up. I've always found women could—that's why I like them. I can walk, talk, swim, drink, do everything else with a man, but walking with a man is not the same as walking with a woman who attracts you physically. Walking with a woman you have no sexual desire for is the same thing as walking with a man— but not so good by a hell of a long way.

Do you understand what I'm trying to say? Why should I want to sail a boat with you? I know lots of men who are really first class shipmates, help one to win prizes, keep one from being drowned, argue with one on art or philosophy, tell blue stories, anything one likes. Do you suppose I want you because you can do all these things better than my men friends? Not dam'd likely. You may do all these things indifferently, even badly, but when you add sexual attraction to them, I prefer you. Which is a very roundabout way of saying that while still being male, if I like you and you say you don't want to do a certain thing—then that thing ceases to exist so far as our relationship is concerned.

The whole explanation of my letter (asking you to come here) is that being human, and having found something that seemed to me to be wonderful, my first impulse was to share it with a person I thought, or rather knew was the most capable of enjoying it and thereby increasing, or rather completing my enjoyment. That, according to my ex- perience of you, was you—according to my experience of you. I couldn't tell what you were thinking about. I don't try to find out. I take you as you are.

Your letter is amusing. You talk as if you were engaged to be married, or hoping to be. Are you? This feeling strikes them all: 'Johnny, I never realised what it meant to feel pure and victorious, till I met her' sort of thing. No, I'm not at all cynical, but it's what happens and the same man, a year later, generally says: 'I love my wife, but oh! you kid.'

Well Meg, whether you're interested practically or theo- retically in the other branches (as the folk would say) of the sport, is your affair. If you had come down to see me, I'd have done anything with you—or if you liked, given you a separate bed and never mentioned the subject at all. Like most women, you think because a man frankly says he wants you, that he has no other interest. Women seem to like being bluffed. Well-I'm interested in you right enough. Seeing you can't see it for yourself, I'd better tell you I suppose . . . and I'll try to help you in any way I can. So good luck to you. Let me know how it goes with you.

I don't see why the School should not be a great success and why you're nervous about paying £100 rent. I was paying £75 by selling pictures. I taught in a school and gave lessons in the studio and no one ever paid a penny for that. Otherwise I'd have made money.

Let me know if you get this letter. I don't know how you're going to find time to wade through it. I intended, like the after-dinner speakers, to say a few words—with the same result. Cheer-oh. Glad to see you're looking fat, don't wear yourself out again.   Yours sincerely, JD

P.S.   I suppose you're in the middle of demenaging, or amenagering, or something of the sort.

P.P.S.   Was it natural for the man (?) Christ to leave his mother (perhaps having been immaculately conceived, it was), remain celebate and prefer dying on the Cross, to being like other people and bringing up a family of useful kids?

Is Nijinski's dancing natural?
Is the 'Sacre' a natural expression of Spring?
Is Botticelli's 'Printemps'?
Is your own dancing natural? If it is, God help you, I can't.
Is anything worth a dam, natural?
Is anything natural worth a dam? Don't bother.
Leave it to the social reformer, he knows all about it.

By the way, wonderful thing 'Carmen'. Heard it by hasard in the gardens the other day.
Isn't 'Carmen' wonderful?

I wonder what I said to suggest I could be contemplating marriage! Nothing was further from my thoughts. I may have mentioned that a very charming man, a Greek scholar who had been a pupil of mine since 1911, still proposed to me every few months, but my one desire was to be with Fergus again. His letters continued:

5th December, 1913. Antibes.
Dear Meg,
    I got your last letter and clipping (which I'm returning in this letter) on the 22nd, having been forwarded from Nice, where I was with Harry McColl. I hope you got my letter, I'm registering this one to make sure. I got your postcard this morning. Of course, yes, I've moved in—been here since the 1st, and until Harry came didn't look up for a minute. I'm very happy, having a great time and am starting to work soon. I began sculpting the other day; the landlord brought me some beautiful clay and it's great sport. You must have a shot at it if you come down. I'm free for Christmas and I'll be very pleased to see you in spite of your sex.
    I was out this morning to the town and it's the most wonderful day imaginable. I can see from the balcony as far as Italy, magnificent huge clouds, clear sky, snow on the Alps, like a beautiful spring day—but I've told you all about it and that you're the only person I want to share it, so if that won't do, go to hell!
    My only pal at present is a praying mantis, a sort of locust artist, quite wonderful. A beautiful green, prays all the time and pays no attention to you walking nearly over him (or her, I don't know). Climbs up the ceiling every now and then and cheerfully falls down with a whack, always in the way, never any hurry, quite a wonderful type.
    Alors, cheer-oh Meg. Let me know at once if you get this letter and if you're coming. The notice is quite good. Didn't D write a notice on you? He writes for the Guardian. Now, reply by return.
                                                    Yours JD

6th December, 1913. Antibes.

Dear Meg,

I got both your letters this afternoon. The prospectuses are splendid; beautiful types you've got. Ann's letter is very good, but then she is really one of the best 'je vous assure'. I suppose she's about as near it as you can get. If you think you've anything to say about women, come along, I've got them pretty well 'considered'. If you can tell me anything, I'll be surprised. I like them very much but for the man who wants anything else, 'women', as such, are ruination—that's to say I, for example, can't use women, and that's why I object to them. My women have never done me any harm, good instead; but look at the people we know. We'll go into it, if you come down.

Harry McColl didn't get married, the doctors said the girl wasn't strong enough. I'm dam glad. Yes, we had a very good time together—walked and talked about everything; it's really a terrific thing friendship. If only one could add sexuality to it without sacrificing one's ideas, but I suppose that's impossible. Of course it is. Harry was the first person to come to see me. He's the man I like best. Quite wonderful.

But what's this you say? You want me for purely selfish motives, you blaguardess. Then your idea is not to devote your life to benefiting me—this is most disappointing. Yes, that's excellent, if we could keep to that, but the real point is that you can come down. Well you know I'll be very pleased, and I'll be all ready for you. Everything is really taking shape at last and high time. So if you decide to come, come as soon as you are free and stay as long as you can. If you have nothing to keep you, you're as well here. Getting here is very simple, you come on to Antibes and I'm about 10 minutes from the station. The thing to do is to travel down from Paris by night I think, starting from the P.L.M. gare. It's a hell of a long way and costs a good deal—and don't forget to take food, there is no dining car or anything on the train. Don't drink the water on the train at any price.

If you're coming, come soon. If not, let me know and I'll

go into this prospectus-sending business and tell you about people by letter as soon as I have time. It would be much better to talk about it.

So Cheer-oh! I must get some dinner now, it's nearly nine o'clock. I've been making a washstand today and haven't had

time to go into town, so I'll have to make soup of onions—there's nothing else. Hell of a life, an artist's. I'll do my best to make you comfortable. You'll have good food, fresh anyway. I'll buy a sack of nuts as soon as I hear you're coming. Bring the articles in magazines on yourself, photographs etc., notices and all that sort of thing—till I see what an ass you are according to the British. Must get to dinner. Look forward to seeing you again.

Yours, best wishes.

Postscript. Monday morning.

I started this letter on Saturday night hoping to post it, then hoped to today, but have worked from breakfast time at a bookshelf and have made something of it. Didn't manage to get into town. Onions finished. Hell.

Well my last letter said something about decent clothes for Monte Carlo, by that I meant merely your ordinary town clothes, nothing special. Here in Antibes you can wear a jersey or anything. Then, can you borrow a kodak, even a brownie?

The place here has given me quite a new start, a different feeling altogether about painting, or rather it has given me what I've been trying to make out of nothing—the colour, the shapes, everything that I was developing by sheer sweat and labour is here. The light that one snatched with excitement when it happened once in a blue moon, is here even in winter.

The weather is wonderful today, like summer. I've been working all day with the doors and windows open. Moonlight nightly. Now I'm going to bed.

The bookshelf is not too bad; things are really beginning to clear up. You never tried joiner work, it's a great trade a carpenter's. What a pity one can't live for a thousand years; from 10 in the morning till one or two in the morning passes like a flash. Life is too short.

Best wishes, yours among the shavings, JD

My first view of palm trees was at dawn in Antibes station
—it will always remain one of my outstanding memories. I
know now that palm trees are not indigenous to the South
of France, but they flourish there and to me they were the
furthest removed from English trees and symbolised everything exotic and romantic that I longed for. When I got out
of the train, there was Fergus taking my bags from me—just
sixty years ago as I write this in 1973.

It is difficult for people who only know that coast *now*, to
realise how wild and unspoiled it was in 1913. The old town
of Antibes, with the Saracen towers, was and still is exactly
the same. The big Place (now Place de Gaulle), with the old
Grand Hotel and the bandstand, was there then, but from this
to the Cap was a common of waste land, with one or two old
villas that are still there. As we walked over the rough ground
the sun rose. It was wonderful. I had my first sight of the
'Phare', the lighthouse that stands on a hill dominating the
whole Cap. It swings its strong beam of light in a complete
circle every few seconds. The Avenue de la Salis is on the
North side of the Phare.

Fergus's little 'hut' enchanted me. It was white-washed
outside and in, with a window on the upper floor, which
had a tiny balcony painted emerald green. From it there was
a distant view of snow-topped mountains, the 'Alpes
Maritimes', now alas called '60–1'! On the other side of the
house was the gate into the garden, also painted green. There
I saw my first fig tree—a splendid specimen, but of course
there were no figs in the winter. There was a vine with
bunches of grapes, and yellow and orange gourds that
climbed all over the trellis Fergus had made for them. The
garden had no palms in it but there were several quite near,
so the Arabian Nights atmosphere was maintained.

The only door into the house opened straight into the
kitchen, with cooking stove, sink and running water.

Christmas Time in the South of France, 1922, Robert Robertson

Beyond was a smaller room which made a dining and sitting room. All the floors were red tiled, so easy to clean, and there was an inside toilet. What more could one want?

In the kitchen a very narrow, ladder-like stair with a hand-rail, led to the upper floor which was divided into two rooms. The smaller just held Fergus's double-bed and the other, with the balcony, *the* sofa already mentioned, his easel and painting things. He had done quite a lot of paintings during the months before I joined him, but was so dissatisfied with them that he had painted them all out. He said they were just *not creative*. When I was around, he spent half the time painting marvellously which delighted me.

The first breakfast is again a vivid memory. Fergus told me to take the bread off the gate and there, literally, the bread was, hanging on the gate-post four small triangular loaves joined together, and below, a bottle of milk. That bread was wonderful, what the peasants eat. Not wholemeal, but grey in colour and free from the German 'improvers' that whiten flour. Fergus put one loaf in front of me and took one himself. I laughed, saying I couldn't possibly eat a whole loaf! He replied, "you soon will" and soon I did. With it we had good French butter, and tea made in a Japanese teapot. I still have a picture in which it figures.

Next, I was given a bath. This was done in the kitchen, Fergus had brought his rubber bath with him and the water could be slopped all over the kitchen floor and then swept out of the front door onto the garden. Having sat up all night in a stuffy 3rd class compartment with wooden seats I was glad of that bath. I then climbed into a clean bed and slept for two or three hours. When I woke it was still only midday!

Fergus prepared an omelette and salad lunch, and later took me for a walk up the hill to the phare. The road was steep and winding, and every few yards there was what looked to me like a little shrine, but was in fact one of the Stations of the Cross. At the top, beside the phare, stood an old church. I believe pilgrims used to climb past the Stations of the Cross on their hands and knees, to reach the little church which is still there in 1973. The views of the whole coast were wonderful.

The furniture Fergus mentions was all made out of the packing cases that brought his stuff from Paris. The bookcase and the washstand I have here now in Glasgow. The washstand is really a work of art. Fergus spent hours on it, painting and re-painting it till he was satisfied and its personality emerged. He felt it had something of an Aztec god about it, and I still feel that. It has much in common with the furniture Mackintosh designed.

This first Christmas at Antibes was truly a revelation, life relieved of obligations! We knew no one, so we were really *free*. We ate, walked and slept, just when we felt like it and never looked at a clock. Every few days we walked into Antibes for provisions. The small épiceries so grandly labelled 'Alimentation Generale' that smelt strangely of spices, oils and coffee, were a delight. There was one called Puigué that sold bunches of freshly dried dates still on their sticks—I have never tasted such wonderful dates. We bought nuts, fresh vegetables, eggs and cheese. Fergus was not a vegetarian by conviction, but as meat and fish were the most expensive food you could buy, he did without, and this suited me perfectly.

One thing that astonished me was that the meals were always the same: *lunch*—porridge, with plenty of milk; *supper*—vegetable soup and an omelette, both meals finished with cheese and fruit as desired. I thought I should get terribly tired of these menus, but of course I made no remarks on them and to my astonishment after a few days I wanted nothing different. Fergus made excellent porridge (he had the meal sent from Scotland), and wonderful omelettes, but

his soups were very dull! Only onions and potatoes with an
oxo cube for flavour. I did ask if I might help by making the
soup sometimes, but he would not hear of it. He insisted on
doing everything himself, saying that I must have a complete
rest, so I did. It was over a year later, when Fergus was living
in London, that one day I brought in a variety of vegetables
and he allowed me to make a soup. He found it so good that
I had to make it ever after!

Fergus insisted on taking a few excursions along the coast,
though I was perfectly happy with our life together,
shopping in Antibes and walking to Juan-les-Pins, or round
the Cap. The big waves breaking on the rocks were
wonderful. In the winter there are terrific storms. The private
bathing places have iron ladders put down each summer,
which are removed and repainted during the winter.

Fergus took me to Cannes to look at the old town and the
harbour. Another day we went to Monaco to see the
aquarium, full of strange fish and underwater creatures and
plants. Finally we went to Monte Carlo. Fergus said all my
friends would expect me to have been to the famous gaming
rooms. I have never had any desire to gamble in any form
and nor had Fergus. We agreed that an artist's life was enough
of a gamble without adding to it, but it was interesting to see
the celebrated gaming rooms, with oil lamps hanging over
each table in case anyone managed to put off the electricity.
The faces round the tables were a tragic study, in which greed
and anxiety predominated. There were a few glamorousfe-
males and smart men as seen on films; but those who struck me
most were the tired middle-aged women and old hags—the
habituées who sat there summer and winter—making notes of
the numbers that came up most often, and working out
systems to break the bank, which of course only broke them.

These regulars fell into two classes: those with money,
mostly old women with hands like claws covered with

diamond rings, and with gigolos if they wanted them. Then those who were dull, respectable-looking females of advancing years who just had the gambling fever. Fergus told me that most of these managed to scrape a very humble living out of their winnings by spending their entire life in those stuffy gambling rooms. What a life—but if that was all they wanted to do, good luck to them! Fergus and I were both glad to get out into the fresh air.

I realised then, and still more now, how good it was of Fergus to take me to Monte Carlo, in which he had not the slightest interest. I appreciated every minute of it, because he was with me. We got a late train back and walked across the waste land in the moonlight to the little white hut, which had become the palace of my dreams.

But this magical holiday soon came to an end. I had to be in London for the opening of the Spring term. I tore myself away in a daze of misery that left no clear memories—except the last, of Fergus standing at the station among the palm trees waving as the train carried me away.

The contrast of London in winter, in those days often enveloped in fog, compared with the sunshine of the south and the sunshine that Fergus brought into my heart was terribly depressing. Luckily I had plenty of classes to teach and problems to deal with.

Fergus's first letter after my arrival in London brought joy and some consolation.

12th January, 1914. Antibes.
Dear Ski,
    I'd just come in from the phare when the facteur brought your card. We've had a gale of wind all day and I went, after porridge which must have been early, round to the rocks. The sea is coming in in great style, really big breakers, emerald green and wonderful white. Then I went up to the phare and thought—'I'll gie in', as they say in Scotland. It was not so

amusing going alone but it was wonderful. The fleet is sheltering on the Juan-les-Pins side—the gale is coming from the South East.

Glad to hear you've laid in a supply of books and pencils. Hope you'll manage to find time to do something when you get back. I think you should keep it up, though it's difficult in London. Glad to hear you paid Kunty, he's a decent chap, though his name isn't so decent. Yes, it really is remarkable how soon one gets into bad habits—I miss you in bed; but the extra knife, fork, spoon, plate, cup, etc., are cleaned and put away. Un pain, un pain du beurre, un litre of milk—one of everything.

I found your yellow Turkish shoes today, by the way—or rather, underneath the sofa. I'll send them with the muffler etc. I see it's six o'clock. I must go into town. We could be in time for Puigué's.

Hope you had a decent passage to London. Best of luck to you.

Yours JDF

I was working on a ballet to three 'Songs of Spring', by Stravinsky. I had met a soprano who was willing to sing them at my little theatre without any fee (I never had any money to pay artists). I had discussed the costumes with Fergus and he said he would do some designs. He sent a rough sketch of my first costume in this letter:

27th January, 1914. Antibes.
Dear Meg, I've been at it since early morning, the most boring bloody job—choosing my drawings and mounts for them and sticking them on the mounts. Hell! So I'm in a very poor state to help you. Specially when it comes to giving something in place of what seemed to be just the right thing. For my part I'd see them in hell. The only thing I can suggest is to have the same thing, but in a dress which you might call "Early Italian"—to suit these refined, cultured people.

You've got too much design on the drawing you sent me, and too many <u>points</u> that fly out. Seems to me you might get the effect more or less of the original idea by a dress like the one I enclose. I don't think the trouser idea is any good as it is, in your drawing. I expected you'd find it would work out differently—the painting of the dresses I mean. But I don't see why it should not be done as well, allowing for translation. I also thought that you might get a blue, in ribbon or cloth or something, better than in paint. I told you in one of my letters, the maroon stuff is just the colour. The blue is too light in the lamplight, make it more the tone of the stuff. If you <u>wet it</u> it comes right.

I'll try to write to some people in Chelsea, but there's not much time, for today is the 27th and I must get my things away. They've to be packed and get to London for frames and be ready for the 18th. So there you are. But cheer-oh! Don't get hysterical, calm yourself. I'll give an introduction to some Chelsea people presently. I'll draw the kind of dress I mean on the inside of the letter. I can't think of anything better. Must go to the gare to find out about rates for grande vitesse. I'd write another 10 pages telling you how much I loved you, but I don't believe you're as much interested in that as the bloody ballet. You have <u>tort</u>. For women, "tout ça ne vaut pas l'amour"—as the song says. All right for men?

27th March, 1914. Antibes.
My dear Ski,

I've just had a good dinner. <u>No</u>! I haven't eaten nuts or dates since you left. I had a wonderful soup tonight, so I'm feeling very contented. I've been working all day in the garden for the last two days. They've planted vines all round and the 'tunnel' and the walls will be covered. The weather is amazing—beautiful clear air, blazing sun and at night the most colossal moon. Really, I want to sleep outside and be out all the time.

There's a big hedge of hawthorn outside, and daffodils growing all round. I made a good sketch that I can paint

1905-1914

from this morning. Then after lunch I lay along on the rocks in the sun till late, then walked round the Cap—so I'm full of health and very contented.

Your drawings are really very good, specially the ink one, I mean as drawings. You really are a most intelligent gosse, and one would think by the drawings, most sensual also. The pencil one too is full of go, and the design at the bottom very amusing. I'm glad to hear you're doing lots of drawings, I wish I could have you with me and work together. It's bloody annoying to be teaching kids. Of course I knew your friend wouldn't like my show. What I was wanting to know was if the "big thing" excited her sensually—touched the spot, so to speak. That was all. I didn't know the drawing was repro-duced in the Art News, though I gave them permission. The picture I'm going to give you, if not sold, is "Winter Gale", the sea through the trees. It's just along where I was lying today, a bit nearer.

I apparently misunderstood Mrs. Alison's letter; but about Simpson, I can't understand at all. If he is so easily offended you're better without him. I thought he was one of my best friends and that sort of thing makes me thoroughly sick of people altogether. I can't be bothered finding out the reason —it might be anything, but he should have replied at least. The best thing is to keep to oneself, unless one has money. By the way, I had a letter from D. She says she was at your show and took friends and found it very interesting, and that she's very keen on dancing. I was going to write to her, but won't now. No one seems to mean it, so to hell with them, so far as I'm concerned.

I won't bore you with drawings or letters, gosse, you've enough to do without such rot. And don't bother about writing unless you want me to do something—though I can't help much as I refuse to write to people when they don't reply.

So cheer-oh! Good luck to you—my best wishes for success.

farewell, Yours JDF

87

It was wonderful getting Fergus's letters. That Christmas at Antibes had shown me all that life could and should be. Yet I had to leave it and return to incessant work and worries, just to keep the School going. Was it worth it—who can tell?

Fergus had a show on in London, I think at the Doré Gallery, and the "big thing" he refers to was the largest picture he ever painted—about 6 × 9 feet—a group of nude men and women dancing among trees and flowers. Many people in those days thought it shocking, though only the backs of the male figures were shown. He called it *Les Eus*— I will quote a note Fergus made about the title—he says it means 'The Healthy Ones' and he invented the word. I think something however must have suggested a foundation for it—he was, as I have said earlier, greatly interested in the derivation of words and always kept Larousse and Skeat beside him for reference.

The friend he mentions in the letter was a very attractive and sensual looking girl, but conventional in outlook. She wanted men to want her, but she didn't want them enough to break with convention and always had marriage in view, which I hope she achieved successfully.

I don't know what happened to the *Winter Gale*, which Fergus says he would give to me. We never gave each other presents at Christmas or on birthdays, but I would love to have that picture if I could find it.

Before I left Antibes I told Fergus about the ballet 'Spring into Summer' that I wanted to do to songs by Stravinsky, in my little theatre. He thought it a wonderful idea and said he would work out designs for costumes, based on Spring in the South—which was already starting: the earth so rich, the colour of ground coffee, you could almost *see* things grow.

Fergus liked my idea for the beginning of the ballet, me almost invisible, sitting on my heels in the centre in an enormous white cloak that covered the entire stage.

1905-1914

Gradually, the first Spring flowers (small children) would creep out from the edges of the cloak—snowdrops, crocuses etc.—then young girls—irises, tulips etc.—would creep out from the cloak and lift the edges of it, to reveal a blue lining; then draw the cloak from me and hang it up behind, making a background, before joining me in a dance of Spring. Finally, the flowers of Summer would dance in from all sides and I'd be crowned with a wreath of upstanding flowers.

1st April, 1914. Antibes.

My dear Meg,

I just managed to finish the colour of the designs tonight before the light went, it's light now till seven. I worked yesterday and all today on them. I hope I haven't kept you waiting, but I've been painting and couldn't settle to them yesterday. I did my best sketch yesterday evening, much the best. What weather this evening after I'd finished—I went out and watered the flowers—they deserved it having sat for the designs. The main design and the earth background one, are from the Girofle in the garden; another of these beautiful "star" flowers has appeared out on the grass. My cherry tree is really a joy, I painted it in my sketch last night. Leaves are coming out on the fig tree—the fig came first, oddly enough. Everything is wonderful.

Well here are the designs, I hope they're some use. The main design you will of course lengthen, broaden, compress or spread; also outline with black or dark brown or blue as you think fit. The centre piece of the back is a pretty complete idea of my idea of it, but one can't tell by small designs. I think the star flower for your forehead is a good idea and you must give the question of size careful consideration. Keep to the direction of the points of the flower and of the leaves in the design—I mean the outlined drawing of course, the other light drawing is just to let you see what the flower is like.

Then the hawthorn and cherry designs you can use on your dress, the hawthorn being white on white dress must be

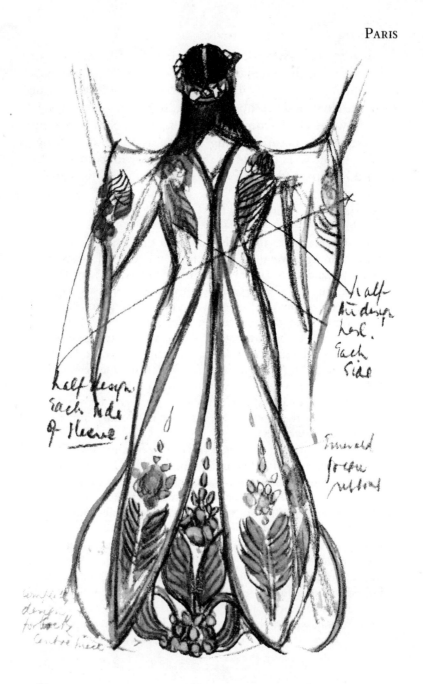

half
the design
here.
Each
side

half design
each side
of sleeve.

emerald
green
ribbons

90

outlined in blue and brown—it should be the bigger of the two patterns. I've done a design with a brown background in case you might want some of the kids to symbolise the earth. Then I'm enclosing your drawings, so I hope one way and another you'll have enough material. I think blue and pink for the kids—I mean so many pink and so many blue, perhaps green, and the earth colour since there are twenty of them. The green would be a darker green but brilliant. I think emerald green is right for you. Then about the blonde wig, I can't see where you get the idea—I mean I can't see the foundation in nature for it; blonde it seems is Summer, you see Spring is hard or strong; it's the struggle; it's the creative impulse, the artist spirit, and is all <u>grip</u> and drawing, definite in drawing, direction, intention. Summer is <u>success</u>, the blonde bourgeoise, arrived, nothing to try for; <u>yellow</u> sunlight, you see, it's woman with children, not the woman hot with passion to have children. No, I think you've missed it. Keep your own hair, as you always wear it, with a wreath round it, it suits you best and it's right for this. Your face should be white and lips full and red—perhaps some red near your eyes.

Then about the ballet—perhaps you have it all settled, perhaps you've done it before, that's the worst of not being able to talk things over; but I have felt this Spring, I've observed it pretty closely as you can imagine, and from the experience my idea of the ballet would be or is, that you should be the "Spirit of Spring", the breath of it so to speak. The kids should express the expressions of it in the shape of flowers (<u>I</u> don't think the $\frac{ground}{earth}$). The ballet should start with all the kids lying absolutely flat, head to the audience, in masses according to colour etc. The music should be intense and suppressed, then you should come on like what Rabbie Burns would call a "gust of joy"—like a whirlwind, to a shriek and blast of the full orchestra, and a flash of following <u>pure white</u> limelight right down to the front, seeming to give full swing to the movement <u>wearing the cloak</u>. Then you should dance round the heaps of kids in and out and round about, so to speak.

... Then they should dance, without you: you off I mean. Then you come on when they stop, all standing in clumps, arms at their sides. You come on without the cloak and dance more as one of them—they having received the breath of Spring and come to life, which—that's to say their relation to you—should express itself by their holding out an arm to you as you come to each group and let them close round you. Then you go off and they dance with more abandon than they did in the first awakening dance. You return in the cloak and dance with them, the whole thing expressing as far as possible, to the utmost, what the French would call l'epanouissement—a wonderful word. All the time they should follow you, I mean one should feel that though they at times go in opposite directions etc., that you are controlling them. This should be expressed by their constant return to a direction which you must make your own and give point to. Then the coda, I believe the musicians call it, should be an absolute and sudden full stop, in which you should come forward, stand both feet together, quite erect and hold up both arms at full stretch—in one hand the white flower, bigger of course than the one in your hair, in order to give it point. Meanwhile the children should also suddenly stop— standing absolutely straight on either side of you, their arms at different angles to express the star shape, or blossoming.

To sum up the different things—first the white flower, star-shaped, that's to say, expanding in all directions, chiefly upward: the longest petal expressing the coolness and cleanness of Spring. Then your cloak, the leaves of it as in the light realistic drawing, song leaves allowing the swing and movement of the Spring wind—and your dancing should be that shape (drawing), but the kids, all angles expressing the straining from one side to the other and upward of the things from the earth—pink being the cherry blossom very simply symbolical, and hawthorn for the others.

Of course there are thousands of other things, but roughly that's my idea, which is entirely from my experience of this

Spring here, and what I have been painting and observing all the time.

Well I suppose you're worn out and I see it's half-past nine, so I must start the soup. I'll send the things tomorrow—I can't tonight because I must register them. Find a minute to let me know by postcard if you get them all right and when you have time let me know what you think of them. I hope they'll be of some use, in any case don't lose them, they might be of some use sometime—I can see possibilities in them. I hope the thing will be a success, hope you're well and all the better of your rest with Simpson and the rest. I could eat one of Mrs. Simpson's dinners just now. Well cheer-oh "She's not a coon as hails from Carolina". Tell me all about your successes, love affairs etc. There's a fine girl in the town here, I don't think she hates me, but you never can tell. She's certainly beautiful. Sorry I'm in this bloody art business—think I must chuck it and start rearing kids. Think I'll come back and do a tour of Scotland to see if there's by chance any of the real thing left, whereby one might breed a race of heroes. I often feel that a little more or a little less and I'd have been a man—might breed a son like the thing. 40 years of art is enough sh., but the "paquet de legumes a un sou", of course. Let me hear how it goes. Hope your face is still fat.

Yours when you need me, JD

That letter is I think one of the most interesting. It shows how uninterested Fergus was in personal recognition or monetary gain, where a question of art that he thought worthwhile was concerned. Yes, he was interested in me, but I know that he would have done as much for *anyone* making as big an effort as I was, for freedom in creative art. It is only possible to show one or two of his designs, but he sent detailed drawings of the Spring flowers in colour.

I kept to my idea of the huge white cloak covering the earth for the opening of the ballet; but followed his idea of very dark hair and the white star-like flower for Spring. As the ballet ended as Summer, I finished however in a wig of gold braid and a wreath of summer flowers, wearing a cloak of gold and brilliant colours.

This ballet was a great success at my Chelsea Club, and I had an offer to perform it in the arena at Olympia during the Spring Exhibition. The offer quite dazzled me, amounting to hundreds of pounds! But when I had paid for orchestration of the music, extra costumes and salaries there was, as usual, nothing left for my production work or personal appearance.

By the time this was over, my mind was fixed on getting back to Antibes *somehow* in the summer, and when it became more feasible a great friend, Eleanor Elder, who started the Arts League of Service, many years before the Arts Council came into being—suggested coming with me as chaperone. It made the trip much easier to explain, and away we went. Eleanor took a room in old Antibes, where she spent much time exploring. Not wanting to dive off the rocks into deep water as Fergus and I did, she bathed every day from the beach near the town and came walks with us round the Cap and up to the phare. We met in Antibes for shopping and sometimes had a meal there, which in those days was very cheap—*no* summer visitors at all and most shops closed.

Eleanor was most tactful, she knew how deeply I loved Fergus by then and how precious every minute alone with him must be. Actually, she had to return to England after two weeks, her mother not being at all well but she agreed not to mention her return as I was determined to stay on for the whole summer holiday.

I have already raved about my Christmas visit to Antibes, but the wonder of the summer at the Cap d'Antibes passes all description. Fergus had everything organised, a good supply of charcoal for slow cooking, omelettes and soups. He had hung a hammock in the fig tree, so one could lie in it and pull the ripe figs—sometimes the early ones dropped on one, overripe!

I am glad to be able to say I *did* appreciate everything to the full; I remember standing on the tiny balcony and saying to myself—nothing can ever *be as perfect as this*—how right I was! We had many many amazing summers later with wonderful friends on the Cap, but none could ever touch that complete isolation and communion on every plane that we enjoyed then—what a honeymoon *should* be, but seldom is!

I was determined to stay till the opening of the School in early September. Fergus was helping me with my painting, in which I was desperately anxious to make some progress. We only went to shop in Antibes once a week and read no newspapers. Life was wonderful.

One day I was sketching the phare, when a gendarme came up and said, "C'est defendu!" I said "Mais pourquoi?" "A cause de la guerre," he replied. Quite innocently, I asked, "Quelle guerre?" At which point the gendarme must have decided I was a nut-case and waved me away. I returned to Fergus to tell him what had happened. "It's the war," he said, "you will have to go back." I did. This was the most devastating experience of my life—I felt literally torn in two. How could I fail my mother and my aunt in this time of crisis? Yet my whole being was with Fergus. With him I wanted to stay, and to help. I can never forget the misery of the parting, when he put me on the train at Antibes, and the terribly slow journey to Marseilles where I was told on arrival that we could not go on to Paris that night. A nice old porter got me a room in a cheap hotel, but when I opened the window, I found it gave onto a narrow corridor—no fresh air at all. But I was dead beat and slept like a log.

The journey to Paris seemed endless. We wandered round France to clear the main lines for troop trains. When we eventually got there, the next question was—could we leave it!

Postcards from Antibes to Paris:

Monday, 7th August, 1914 (5 o'clock)
Just received your two cards of the 4th. Hope you got mine.
Hope you got away. I think you should, things, as I thought,
have changed for the better—according to the papers, the
Germans have left Paris. Naturally I can't say how hellishly
annoyed I am about everything, but what can one do? Let me
know immediately if you need money. I've given you all the
other help I can think of in my postcards. I'm working every
day (and I'd have helped you with your painting if you'd
been here) oddly enough in spite of being very worried
about you. But news that the Germans left, was comforting
last night. Cheer-oh. You'll get away all right. They seem to
be going further away, according to the papers today. I'm
studying them every day. Calm yourself, getting excited
doesn't help anyway. You'll get away soon—best wishes
old dear,   yours, JDF

Saturday, 5th September (12 o'clock noon)
Got your postcard of the 2nd this morning, and your <u>two</u>
wires about an hour ago. Am going into the town to wire to
tell you to go to Cook's Office, Place de l'Opèra, for all
advice and information. Sorry Harry is away, dam'd luck;
just sent him a card. Hope you get away, but if you see that
you can't <u>definitely</u>, I'll wire money at once. Tell them at
the hotel that you know me—the manageress knows me, if
it's the same one. In case of trouble go to the British Consul
in rue Faubourg St. Honoré, just behind the Marigny
Theatre. Let me know <u>at once</u> if you <u>really definitely can't
get away</u>. Perhaps better come back here in that case, but
make absolutely sure first. No!! Better in Paris, you're at
least near home—perhaps might get away to Dieppe, then
across somehow. Ask your mother to ask influential people
at home. I'll try to think of someone I know in Paris. I'll
send you another card this evening if I can think of anyone,

Log Cabin Houseboat, 1925, Scottish National Gallery of Modern Art, Edinburgh

or if I have any useful idea. Cheer-oh! I think there may be a sudden change in affairs in a day or two—I mean for the better. In any case, there's nothing to do.

Saturday, 5th September, 1914 (6 o'clock)
Dear Meg, I sent you a postcard and a wire today about 1 o'clock. Of course I don't know what to think. I thought you'd better go to your aunts in Dieppe; then, you wouldn't be able to get to the Boulogne or Dover boats, if there were any by chance, so I thought you should come back here; but that doesn't seem the right idea either, unless it's certain that you're going to be shut up in Paris—in that case you'd better find out, by going to Cook's or the British Consul, if you are going to be shut in and in that case leave, and we'll try to get back by boat. If you need money I'll wire it (you've got papers to show at the Post Office). I hope you manage to get away on Monday, but rather than be shut up in Paris, come back here. Don't let yourself be shut in if you can get away. Perhaps Dieppe would be better—here, you're so far away. Make a dive for Dieppe if your aunts are there. I think that's best. But here rather than Paris; and go to Cook's or the Consul. Have nothing to do with strangers. Ask about trains for Dieppe and here, and if they are likely to be stopped.
Cheer-oh dear, JDF

Saturday 5th September, 1914 (7 o'clock)
Just had dinner and am going to town to post these cards. I've been thinking of people in Paris. Go to the rue Boissonade and ask for Mme. Bosch—say she's a friend of Miss Archibald and Mr. Madariaga. She used to be in the part on the right side that goes back, a sort of a court, used to be a nunnery. Ask the concierge at the left corner of the street. Then there's a Russian sculptor, Aronson, 93 rue de Vaugirard, a great friend of Rutter and acquaintance of mine—very decent. Then an artist friend of mine, Rupert Bunny, 10, Avenue

Charles Floguel. Then Mrs. Robson, 1 Place Wagram. A Mexican artist (afraid he's away) Zarraga, 4 rue Coetlogon, off the Boul' Raspail, near the Hotel Lutetia. Then a journalist, Jules Paublan, 278 Boul' Raspail. Mme. Bosch first; next Aronson, Bunny, Robson, Zarraga—no, Zarraga second. Paublan I don't know much about, but he might help you. Be careful of mixing with people you don't know. I thought of sending some money by wire, but you might have gone before it got there. I got your card and postcard and replied to home. Anyone having read this card could appear to know you there's too much information on it, so be on your guard. Wire if you are leaving.

In Paris I was really very lucky. I stayed two nights with a cousin of my mother's, and was then told there were trains to the coast from the Gare du Nord, though of course no guarantee when boats would leave for England. I took my hand luggage—all I had—to the station and to my amazement was pushed into a train for Boulogne that was just leaving. It ran onto the quay and there was a boat, the steam coming out of its funnels! "Hurry, hurry," everyone called —I did, and just made it.

There were not many passengers. We were given life-jackets and told to put them on, but nothing happened. The sea was calm and I suppose I should have felt relief when my feet were again on English soil but I only felt utter desolation, for my heart was still with Fergus in Antibes. I tried to share in the joy my mother and aunt felt on getting me back. They were very tolerant about Fergus, but I knew that had we been legally married, they would have accepted that my first duty was to stay with my husband. To me, Fergus was my man for ever—ceremonies and legal documents meant nothing to us. Further word from Fergus just kept me going—

Wednesday, 16th September, 1914. (5 o'clock) Antibes to London.

Just got your card. No, don't want anything furnished, seems reasonable all the same. You can imagine the amount of furniture I will bring. Want a studio I can sleep in. Still packing. Don't pay any attention to what people say about painting. Keep at it, that's all. Splendid weather here, damson jam sounds cheering. Keep a lookout for an unfurnished studio. Yes, try painting heads. Hope Guinness isn't up in price.   Cheer-oh.   JDF

25th September, 1914 (5 o'clock) Antibes to London.

Just got your two letters—a week to get here. The packing has been a hell of a job, chiefly because I'm doing it very thoroughly, and up to now it's certainly a masterpiece. Tomorrow or the next day will finish it, then I must arrange about sending, so I expect to leave at the latest about the middle of next week. Then I think Harry McColl will be in Paris, so I'll stay a day or two if he is. Then on. Glad to hear the painting is going strong—am anxious to see it. EG seemed to be the right sort; a very decent offer—something like a pal. The frames seem to be very cheap if they're good. The fountain idea is most cheering—I'd like to bathe in it today —need a lot of it to make up for this packing business; very fit all the same. Glad you are, I'll be there before the 16th I hope. Hope by that time you've had real luck—patriotism is a good thing, but it shouldn't 'empêche' other things. So cheer-oh. Still figs on the tree, very juicy now.   JD

How I longed to be with Fergus in Antibes helping him to pack up and crate his things. He said I was a good 'mate', handing nails, pliers, etc., at the right moment. To do everything single-handed must have been a great strain—then, giving up the little home and lovely garden he had made, when he had hoped to settle there for life was a sad disillusionment. Instead he was forced to go to London, which he hated.

At last the packing was done and I found a note he made about his departure: Catch the last Japanese boat to London for my furniture. Chased out of the house by neighbour's dog barking. Good luck disguised.

His journey to Paris was worse than mine. I think it took two days and nights from Marseilles to Paris in crowded wooden-benched carriages, but Fergus said the people were wonderful, everyone shared the food and drink they had with them. They sang and slept as they could. At last Fergus arrived in Paris and there spent several days with Harry McColl, one of his greatest friends—till he was able to get a boat to England.

LONDON 1914~1925

At last Fergus got to London. I had found a furnished room for him in Paulton Square from which he could look for an unfurnished studio or flat.

He was never keen on a purely North studio light as he considered it too cold. He liked the sunlight coming in. His furniture could not arrive for a month at least, so he came to our flat for his main meals, and much appreciated my mother's French and English cooking. He took to my aunt at once though her outlook was really diametrically opposed to ours. Kathleen Dillon was living with us at that time and starting to help me with the teaching.

Fergus was delighted with the school and theatre premises. We had the whole floor of a building 100 feet long, with a stone staircase at each end and proper exit doors with bars that pushed outwards. We had divided one end into dressing rooms and wardrobe; the stage was in the middle, raised seating for an audience was at the other end.

Fergus entirely approved the way I ran the Club. We met on the 7th, 14th and 21st of each month. The 7th was always a performance of original dances and costumes; the 14th was a discussion night—someone opened it with a short talk, and then it was a free-for-all discussion with no chairman. Great fun and often very interesting. The 21st was a purely social event at which we danced to records and had a buffet supper. The Goossens family were great supporters. I can't remember how we contacted them, but Eugene, Lèon and Sidonie were constantly with us and always ready to give their services, to play for dances and ballets. Marie came only occasionally. Eugene became one of Fergus's great friends because of his interest in the relationship of the arts. Boonie (Eugene's wife at the time) was a very good cellist and always willing to play for us. Fergus and Anne Estelle Rice designed and painted costumes and backcloths for us—often into the night and receiving no payment.

The Club certainly drew together an amazingly varied collection of people. Among the painters, writers and musicians were Augustus John, Epstein, Wyndham Lewis, the Sitwells, Arnold Bax, Gordon Craig, Ezra Pound and others. Officers of the French army got to know of this Club and became regular visitors. I remember especially a Colonel Boileau, who got me to do a ballet to a poem, *En allant vers la Ville*, by a friend of his for which I also composed the music. Then there were doctors, scientists, mathematicians, and astrologers, who gave interesting talks. C. K. Ogden, who originated Basic English and had done translations, gave Fergus a copy of one of these—the philosophy of 'As If', by Wienhanger, which interested Fergus enormously. They became great friends.

After much looking around, Fergus took a first floor flat at 14 Redcliffe Road. There was a large front room with a balcony over the porch, folding doors to a back room and a kind of conservatory on the half landing with a gas cooker, a sink and just enough room to use his rubber bath. The front room made a good studio, but had to be heated by a coal fire.

Kathleen Dillon was the first of my pupils that Fergus wanted to paint, and I quote now from notes about Celtic Design that he wrote much later, in which he mentions the two paintings he made at that time and eventually gave to her:

> When I came back to London at the beginning of the first world war in 1914, I met one of Margaret Morris's best pupils, Kathleen Dillon, a very good looking, charming and intelligent girl—naturally I wanted to paint her and she posed for my 'Simplicity'. One day she arrived with a remarkable hat. I said, 'that's a very good hat you've got.' She said, 'Yes! isn't it? I've just made it.' It was just like a rose, going from the centre convolution and continuing the 'Rhythm' idea developed in Paris and still with me. Looking at K I soon saw that the hat was not merely a hat, but a continuation of the girl's character, her mouth, her nostril, the curl of her hair— her whole character—(feeling of her) like Burns's 'love is like a red red rose'. So she like Burns again, lighted up my jingle and I painted 'Rose Rhythm'—going from the very centre convolutions to her nostril, lips, eyebrows, brooch, buttons, background cushions, right through. At last, this was my statement of a thing thoroughly Celtic.
>
> 'Kathleen' is Irish, in the Celtic referred to as 'Dillion son of the Wave', and the movement was a wave movement— and was a movement not only in the hat she had created, nor in my picture, she created it in herself through and through, which was evident in all her dances we had the good fortune to see in MM's theatre at Flood Street, Chelsea.

I composed a dance I did with Kathleen to a toccata and fugue by Bach which was a tremendous success at our Club, but got no further. Fergus spent hours rehearsing us and designing the costumes. They were diamond shapes of different colours stitched onto flesh coloured vests, and on our legs and arms held in position by very thin elastic. Finally Fergus pronounced the dance 'a masterpiece'—it was repeated many times.

I don't remember who introduced Angus Morrison to me. Getting pianists to play for the classes was always a problem, the usual hack pianists who played 3-time or 4-time for the usual ballet classes were hopeless. Somebody brought this slim boy of only 14 to play to me. He was amazingly good and could read anything at sight. I of course engaged him at once. I had composed each exercise to a tune by Schubert which expressed the mood and the way the movements should be done. Fergus had a great admiration for Angus as a boy, because he appreciated this approach to music for exercises, which certainly had not been done before, and soon he became the pianist for our Club Shows as well as for classes.

Angus had a very beautiful sister, Olga, a few years his senior, who came to my classes and took part in performances. Fergus did many drawings and also painted her; she had a good voice and sang at some of our shows.

Fergus agreed at once to take the painting classes for our students and also the children. It was Fergus's idea, in 1914, that everyone could benefit by trying to draw and paint on free lines (now in 1973 this is generally accepted). In particular, he believed *all dancers* should study design and colour in relation to costumes and decor—but this has not yet been accepted.

Fergus came to all our Club lighting rehearsals. At that time among our pupils were Angela and Hermione Baddeley, Penelope Spencer, Elsa Lanchester and Elizabeth Ainsworth, now Cameron, who was very intuitive in regard to Fergus and could tell us what he would say about the lighting before he said it. He had infinite patience and would spend hours to get the best possible effect with the means at our disposal.

So the first year of the war passed quickly, and did not affect us much. An occasional zeppelin passed over, but we just carried on.

With the arrival of summer in 1915, Fergus thought he should go to Scotland and see his mother and sisters living outside Edinburgh, also Peploe and his oldest friend, Ressich, who lived in Glasgow. Of course I missed him terribly but he wrote to me when he could.

His first letter—

Tuesday, 10 August, 1915. Edinburgh.

Dear Gosse,

I went into town today to see Peploe. Ressich arranged for us both to come to Glasgow to see him. I got no reply at the house so I suppose he's away. I got your letter. Yes, I'm in the bosom of the family right enough and it's not so bad. They're really very happy healthy people. As I said, there's a kid staying here with the mother. The gosse is a great kid, very much the same sort of state as Angel, but more lively.

The country round about is very good. I'm going to make sketches, so you'll see later. My sister has a very good head to draw. I was at the tailor's today, so may get a new suit and be able to appear in public.

Today in town, having some time to wait, I went to see Jean. She was out so I talked to her mother for about an hour and a half. Most extraordinary experience. I've told you before how wonderful I thought the old lady—well, we talked about one thing and another and—à propos being unable to remember a man's name—she quoted the Holy Fair: the beginning of it, and started to tell me how wonderfully real it was. Then told me all about holy fairs; how people brought their own chairs, and the lads and lassies at the back and so on; and what a wonderful man Burns was; how I really couldn't appreciate him because I'd never lived the life she had; and finished up by saying, 'It's a' a masterpiece'; then 'Death and Dr. Hornbook'—how 'wonderful real' the part was when he was staggering along; then about Burns's 'glorious independence'—how the present generation seemed to have lost the idea and 'got nothing in its place but cinemas'.

All this she told me of her own bat—told me as one speaks to a person that belongs to some unfortunate class degenerated from all that's worthwhile. I assure you it was a wonderful experience. The old lady sat there and talked till she disappeared in the dark as the twilight changed to night. Then she lit the gas to show me some ginger jars and a beautiful old chest of drawers belonging to the Burns period of her life. I said nothing all the time, for a dam'd good reason—I didn't feel a giant when I left, but I felt a very cheerful small boy. Wonderful.

Well, dear Gosse, I got your letter and am glad you're getting on a-collecting some fat and am sorry not to have written to you sooner.

I wonder if I told you in the first part of the letter that I looked for a (copy of) Burns and saw nothing special—will look again tomorrow. I go into town again to meet Peploe. I didn't go through to Glasgow and Ressich got more leave and comes on Saturday, but Peploe came through and I met him at the train.

I have started drawing again, apple trees etc.; and the flapper took me golfing the other day. A very nice course just near. She also takes me walks—she's really a fascinating kid, and it amuses me to watch myself in her company. She's quite difficult to understand, seems the Angel sort at times, but again, doesn't. A complete artist in the sex attraction business, yet apparently a kid; then very cynical—extraordinary. Quite amusing, or rather I am, alongside her.

We're having thunderstorms and deluges of rain, so the sculpture is not going so strong and the Peploe-Ressich business has broken in. I got the note enclosed from Angel. I wrote to her to come to see me.

Did I tell you that I thought your drawings very good, but they need more point—they're too much all-over the same, like a background. It is a central thing of some sort that is needed, or if not central, dominating. But more of that later. I'll send you some photos perhaps—it's about three in the morning, so must shut up as I've to be in town in the morning.

So cheer-oh, Gosse, I miss you tremendously. Good luck Maggie darlin', let me know how things are going.

Yours JDF

Your drawing of us taking porridge off the 12ft block is very amusing.

It was over a month before I got the next:

27th September, 1915. Edinburgh.
Dear Gosse,

Sunday is the limit; and next worst nuisance is printing photos with paper I used yesterday. I nearly went mad trying to get them flattened out. Today, when dry, they were rolled up to about the size of a toothpick, and by the time I got them straightened out they broke or tore, so the fruits are not great, m—de!

Talk about your financial worries—yesterday was the limit. Cold, bleak, pouring rain, so I managed to get these prints done—took all day. This feeling of Sunday. A good enough day of course for painting, drawing, bed or the sofa before the fire in the studio, but otherwise, my God! I tried going a walk the other Sunday, but people made me want to blow hell out of everything. In their Sunday clothes and faces to match—again a shower of M...s! Today I got back to the sculpture, not so bad. Very cold, wonderful moon tonight. Lately huge moon; great harvest here, fine crops and good weather. Have been out at night looking at the fields, the country is splendid in movement—really amazing.

Altogether, the place since I came has been delightful because of the weather, the people, the village blacksmith (I took my chisels to him tonight), the joiner, the builder—all of these people are most human and sympathetic.

The other morning my sister burst into my room about 8.30 to say that the coalman had arrived (I work in the part of the garden where the cart comes in, right in the middle of the 'drive'; not carriage drive, coal-cart drive). I said hell!!!! of course, because I'd stuck the head of my mother on a base of cement. I thought of the coalman. I dressed and my sister said the man had put my stuff to one side . . . ! I rushed down, here was a splendid looking giant, very good looking, he said good morning and, 'I moved them, they're all right, very interesting, very good carving, I lifted it up a bit and looked at it.' He looked more like a sculptor than I do, by a long way, oh yes! Had seen what it was—the head of my mother. He'd lifted it by the bottom so it couldn't be damaged. I lifted it later and broke the cement. He's a great chap. So is the man I bought the stone from. All that is dèja quelque-chose, n'est pas? I said to the coalman, 'Stone carving is most interesting.' He said, 'Yes, and you've got such a fine place to do it in', which was a marvellous thing to say, for it's the place that makes me do it. Seeing things against the foliage.

Well, I hope you find the photographs interesting. I'll have some of the garden etc. to show you when I see you. I hope you have a good voyage to H and will benefit from the stay. You should keep drawing when you have the chance. Well Maggie darlin' I'll shut up now. I've not given you much news or amusement, but what can you expect—I'm thinking of nothing but the stone cutting. It's a great business, I tell you. If one could get at it under real conditions: I mean a private place and soon. Certainly, here, everything is helping that can help, but there are always things wanting.

Let me know your plans. I'll be back soon, I can see—for the weather is getting too cold to work outside and there's nothing to do indoors that I can't do better in London.

Cheer-oh, yours JDF

Apparently Fergus stayed on in Scotland longer than he had intended—

Sunday, 10th October, 1915. Edinburgh.
Dear Gosse, here are the drawings. They are masked 1, 2, 3, etc., in order of merit.

The first is the best because the lines you have, express form, and the effect is living. The composition is good because it has balance and allows one to see the effect of the whole thing, instead of distracting attention by some disjointedness or bad distribution of interest. The second has the same qualities and the third the same, but less successful. The third is, as I told you, not good enough in the shadows—by that I mean that the shadows do not amplify or supplement the outlines, but rather (through want of being 'right', and as understood and as expressive as the outlines), detract from the whole. The hair over the brow is good, at the right side of the head. The shadow is no good. The fifth drawing is weak in distribution of darks. The sixth, rather good for form, but anaemic. Seventh, thin, not bad in contours. Eighth, weak; ninth same; tenth undecided—want of tones and selection. Not seen.

The first is really excellent, not because it is in outline, but because the outline is good. You might have quite the same effect with every complete drawing. See what I mean? Anyway I think it is first class. Keep at it.

The widows drawing was most impressive—the distribution of the yellow and pink and seen through, the flesh, was really tremendously successful. Colours of the curtains expressed the folds of curtains—excellent design and colour scheme kept and helped the excitement and movement of the figures and state of mind, both by the folds and of course the design. By the way, I think the pinks, dark and light, with gold or red surrounding, made a very good colour pattern.

The movement of the figures and action of the Months' necks, heads etc., was a complete success in expressing what one feels when in the swim, and one writes of the condition. It certainly is a great business—besides, the colour scheme was quite the colour of feeling of colour, or the sensation of colour one feels mixed with, when in the extasy of it, if you see what I mean. And all of this, seems to be a matter of getting the right thing, which I think we may reasonably call art—what accuracy doesn't give; that is to say accuracy in the

ordinary sense, for you have to be <u>accurate</u> or <u>true</u> to your
<u>feeling</u>, inspiration or whatever you call it, otherwise it is
bloody slop, without guts or organisation. The person doing
it may have all the accuracy, guts, organisation, or may
claim he has, that's not the affair of the spectator—his affair
is to see if the work got it. To find a real basis for saying it
has or it hasn't, is of course a big job—and having found it,
to express it is another. So here we are again, however, I
think that a lot of your things do get it. This drawing, to a
great extent, and many others of the same order, which I
have kept and will be cheered to see again—the drum ballet
and the 'Idol' and the dance with K, certainly got it.

This has been Sunday, and being a dull day I've been
packing. I hope you're comfortable and getting good food
and enough. See you do—you're not going to get much more
than porridge when you come to see me. Hell of a job, this
keeping well. I'm on stout, great stuff. Stout and plenty of
meat, great life, I wish I had it always. Good bed also. Sleep
like a rock, but the days are getting too short and the weather
too uncertain, so I feel I want to be back in a place of my own
to potter about.

Cheer-oh, Gosski, I didn't intend to write to you tonight,
had plenty else to do. Regards to M, is she having a lash at
the sulphur etc.? Let me know in time when you're going,
so that I won't be sending letters too late.

JDF

Fergus's next letter I think is wonderful, though I am a
'squeamy veg', I can appreciate it aesthetically.

19th October, 1915. Edinburgh.
Dear Gosse . . .My God, let me have artists for friends—I
mean people who feel, even if they're grocers, coal-heavers,
anything you like except people devoid of sense of time,
colour and sound.

The man I called on, on Sunday night, was discussing
painting and has a real feeling for it. I mentioned Burns (of

course) and he told me he was at a Golf Club dinner and a butcher who was a great admirer of Burns recited 'Address to a Haggis'. He put so much into it that he nearly collapsed at the end.

Being a squeamy veg, of course you'll think that most ludicrous and disgusting. I think it splendid and inspiring. The man making haggis, selling haggis and reciting the haggis address with real feeling of sympathy with Burns's understanding and sympathy, seems to me to be really getting near the real thing. I'm sorry you can't see it. Think of this disgusting person, a dealer in meat! Worse still, a dealer in tripes—that is, entrails, innards, or guts. A stuffer of tripes, entrails, innards or guts. A maker of haggises, or haggi. That is, a person who stuffs intestines of animals with chopped livers, in fact the large and small stomach-bags of sheep, stuffing them with a mixture of lights, liver, heart and oatmeal, Jamaica peppers and black peppers and salt and the juice the pluck was boiled in, stirrrred into a consistency and stuffed into the large stomach-bag, sewn up with a needle and thread and boiled for hours and prodded from time to time with a large needle—to let out the gas and keep it from bursting.

Imagine him over a cauldron of boiling haggises, watching them and prodding them with a needle, moving them about rhythmically while Burns's words run in his head and at moments of intense emotion, at the sight of their fullness of form and the knowledge of their fullness of food, of real food that nourishes both through feeling and fact—at these moments, feeling the continuity of idea that comes from having conceived created and completed the work—at these moments this frightful person will get into the fourth dimension, so to speak, and recite with the fullness of emotion derived from this comprehensive experience, marking the rhythm with the needle, and punctuating the time with prods.

The uncouth poem of the haggis-fed ploughman, my dear Margaret, is enough to make anyone brought up decently on

Plato (à l'anglais) vomit. In fact no one but Chaucer, or a
butcher, or JDF could be expected to stand it. Don't tell any
of your friends you know anyone who knows about this.
Destroy this letter at once by burning the cochon! Think of
him perspiring.

Well, can quite see why the man Burns isn't much talked
about in polite society. In the Everyman edition I bought for
you, the complete reply to the tailor appears—and it wouldn't
do. It's not complete in the Tauchnitz.

What a terrible thing it is for a man to express his feelings
freely about anything that moves him to express himself.
This war is all right, but to think a man should take it on
himself to express what he thinks, is outrageous. Anyway,
we're fighting for freedom, that's always if we win we shall
be free to be anything but frank. If France wins, artists will
be free to be frank. In Burns's time it was pretty bad. Fancy
Burns up before the 'Kirk Session'—Good God.

If this war doesn't settle this so-called 'Christian' tyranny,
it's a failure, whatever the result. I can agree that no price is
too high, if the world could be reasonably rid of, or free
from this paralysing hypocracy, but suppose it is really the
backbone of the nation? When you hear that men at the
front—in the Dardanelles for example—submit to being told
by some missionary or parson that they can't play the piano
on Sunday, must only sing hymns, there's nothing to do but
give up.

But must shut up, Maggie darlin'. Sorry to inflict all this
on you—effects of the wet weather.

Yours JDF

In 1916 I got the idea of having a Summer School, in some
spot where classes could be out of doors, with sea bathing,
walks, discussions and social dancing in the evenings. In 1973
this idea hardly sounds original as summer schools are held
for pretty well every subject!

I thought North Devon sounded attractive, rugged

The Picnic, n.d., Mr. and Mrs. Ian Robertson

country but trees growing down to the sea. My mother and I decided to try Combe-Martin, then a tiny fishing village. We got some rooms at a very small cost and took Kathleen Dillon with us (hence the 'K' Fergus refers to in his letters).

Monday, 7th August, 1916. London.

Dear Gosse,

I'm glad to hear that you got there without bursting your chin strap or something like that, and the thing seems all right, but the bathing . . . certainly be careful, watch the tide and don't twist your hip getting to the beach. You had luck for a day to go down. It was cold here. I hope you're none the worse of the day at the busses cooking dinner etc.—if so, you may be glad to hear that the thing I was working on is much better. Very like you and very solid. In fact I think quite good. I worked on it all next day and on and off till yesterday about one o'clock, when I was eating apples on the balcony. Looking up the road, two very decent looking types turned the corner. Very good looking legs. I wondered where they'd sprung from. Very good looking dresses etc. Presently, they waved and turned out to be Ruby and Elsie. Ruby looking very well. So they stayed a bit, then I went to lunch and tea. At night to Marriots—except for that, I'd have packed, but being all dressed up, had to go somewhere. I've to dress up and go to the bank today; and see about trains. I think I'll go on Thursday—Elsie wants to bring someone on Wednesday afternoon and P comes tomorrow. She was here on Saturday and I made some very good drawings of her, before and after tea; both great successes.

Now I must get ready and get into town and get back to the packing. I'm very well indeed. Hope you are. Best wishes to you all—I'm much relieved to hear the place is a success.

Yours JDF

The next letters are from Edinburgh, where Fergus had gone to stay with his mother and sisters.

20th August, 1916. Edinburgh.

Dear Gosski,

The weather is as cold as November and poured torrents for the last 24 hours. Terrible. We have a fire on tonight and much need, I tell you.

I've read all the Tatlers and find the world consists of the stage and society—which makes me feel rather out of it. I think after all I'd rather be Mrs. Raymond Hitchcock and be all dressed up. Clothes seem to be the important thing—or as the warriors call it, 'kit'. I'd come to the conclusion that clothes (especially after the last month or so in London) were a dam'd nuisance for anything that matters—and specially for that which matters most. But I seem to have got side-tracked, as the Americans would say. They certainly were a dam'd nuisance the other day—I had to wear two pairs of trousers at the sculpture business, it was too cold with the thin ones except as overalls. I've been at it two afternoons and have done three sides of a stone, nearly square. It resembles somewhat the one you've seen. Same kind of stone too. I hope to finish it tomorrow and take some photos, which I'll send you if they're worthwhile.

The sculpture on the whole is going very well—except that I've had some bad luck with the stone. Very hard in places and sometimes soft. The new stand I made is quite a success: higher, and more rigid. It certainly makes a difference to have a good stand. It was a sort of brown terracotta colour, so I painted it white and with the rose coloured stone on the top, it looks well. Tell K I'm putting the feeling of the last time I saw her, into my sculpture—full and round.

Cheer-oh.

1916 Edinburgh.
Dear Gosse,

I sent you a card. When I'd read your letter I went to the Gardens and could hardly find a space on the grass. Soldiers' and girls' shapes everywhere. As I've always said, it's quite a good place if one had somewhere to go. There were quite a lot of good types about, so you can imagine the effect of your letter, which was most cheering and interesting. I finished the block and took the photos into town, but brought

them back. I couldn't have them done so I don't know what to do—they're nothing extraordinary but too much for these people.

I'm being well fed and the garden is charming and now the weather is so splendid, if I had you people to share it, it would be great. The people are very nice of course, but it's not enough. In short, it's a mistake. You're certainly lucky you two and ought to enjoy your holiday—what freedom. I'm on my guard every minute and there's no one I can speak to. I certainly am wasting a great percentage of energy in the most stupid way.

I got your picture postcard. The place seems most interesting—have you tried bathing yet? It's a pity you couldn't get a quiet corner for sun baths and revel in the heat-wave if it comes.

Your drawing of the valley is very good, and as you say, I'm glad you learned in time so as to make the most of the opportunity—but <u>study</u> it, don't rush at it, and <u>don't</u> m'a-tu-vu <u>unconsciously</u>. I certainly hope you will, for me. I hope you're getting plenty to eat—plenty cream I suppose. Glad K has done a good drawing. Tell her to keep at it—as you know, there's no better practice than that sort of drawing. Give her my love and same to you.

Cheer-oh. Yours JDF

August 26th, 1916. Edinburgh
. . . Hope the show was a success. I'm going to see Peploe and may go with him to the Simpsons, so don't write till I let you know. The weather at present is hopeless and there's nothing to do. If it keeps up I'll go back to London . . . of course won't go to the Simpsons if it's like this—can't go anywhere but to bed . . .

August 30th, 1916. Edinburgh.
Dear Gosse,

I was in town the other day and got your letter—the one with K's drawings in it. They're very good and the abstract one suggests most things; the other is full of movement. I'm glad the show was a success and that you had a decent man to play—give him all the news about modern music you can, it's important to a man having to stay 'out of things'. I'm glad you'll be able to bathe. The weather here has done it thoroughly, rained without a stop for three days and four nights; and after doing it for another day with stops, dried up and is now as good as anywhere in the world. Cold but splendid, so I worked about seven and a half hours on the head of K, which is nearly finished. After dinner had a good walk—yes, the country is wonderful in fine weather. If one had a house by the sea, a decent climate and a 'partee carre', it would be all right—even three would be pretty good, but freedom of course. Think the town is best on the whole, while the wet weather was on. For example, I had nothing to do— there's nowhere to work unless outside, so I was sick of it. You and K are lucky indeed—

Sunday September 3rd, 1916. Edinburgh.
Dear Gosse, how goes it? I hope the weather is not like we have—pouring torrents all day, dark and a Sunday. This is a wonderful climate—it's been not so bad last week and by working seven or eight hours a day, I just managed to get the head of K nearly finished last night—a superb night—it had got nearly dry and looked very well. This morning very wet again. Fool, I'd hoped to get it photographed while dry —well, it's worse—well, it's worse in the trenches. Last week I was cursing the weather and my sister explained that the weather was for people who read, went to cinemas and had a hobby to pass the time indoors—of course I couldn't explain that I agreed about the indoor hobby; well of course a wet Sunday is not so bad for you—in your place I could amuse myself very well.

I woke this morning feeling very fit. After breakfast I took as long as possible to shave, then had a warm bath which I revelled in, then a cold bath and rub down—and I'll leave you to picture it. Glad to hear you and K are getting fat.

I'm going into town soon and hope to hear from you. When I was out walking last night, I thought how wonderful it would be if we were all on good terms and in Paris. We must, as soon as possible—for awhile anyway. There's no doubt life as I was living it before I left to come here is the right thing—only, one should start as soon as possible and have plenty food and a decent climate. Let me know how long you intend to stay. I could be very happy if the weather was good—if I can work, it's all right.

JDF

17th September, 1916. Edinburgh.
Dear Gosse . . . I went to see S but the weather being unsuitable, I didn't stay till dark. Came home for dinner very late; went for a turn till train time and arranged for Tuesday. Free conversation anyway. I'm glad you've been working and if the drawings are as good as the coloured ones you sent, they'll do. If they're suitable, a very good dance might be made of the ones you sent. See that you don't rush at the thing with a yell—take your time.

Today is a mess of wind and rain. Very cold and miserable —can't go out, so am writing after lunch. Generally do it after dinner. I tried the writing business, but the house is too cold during the day. Fire on today. And at night, people just at your elbow. Couldn't do it. Can't do anything surrounded by people. Just now I'd like to do some drawings—no, it's out of the question. Really, complete freedom is a rest. I certainly revel in it when I have it. Hope we may get there sometime.

I'm looking forward to seeing you again with P and hope for developments, I think it ought to be all right. Your holiday progress has been a great success—the three must have been amusing. Certainly T is great value—give her my regards. I can imagine the song and the film play are amusing. I'm very glad to hear about David—very good news. Give her my best wishes and let me know when she's going away . . .

. . . I'm going to Glasgow on Tuesday and will stay some days. I had intended to go today, so you can send letters there—c/o Ressich, 13 Grosvenor Crescent. Take the address, I will let you know when I am coming back. I think I'll be in London by the 10th or so—the weather is still very dizzy . . .

K and Mrs. seem to be having a great time, I'm very glad the old lady is enjoying herself. You seem to have had a great time at D's—there's no doubt, comfort is the right idea —there's plenty of the other thing to be had easily. Yes, it seems a waste, but you'd need to know what were the ideas on the subject, of course maybe the opposite of ours—but they don't expect you to have the ideas of the Bishop of London thank God—but that brings me to the point of censoring according to the Bishop of London and General Smith-Dorrien: I should say that in order not to corrupt the minds of the 'boys', as he, the bishop, endearingly calls them the 'little dears', the only things you can produce are East Lynnes and Sign of the Cross's; H.M.S. Pinafore is all right, it appears; the result of the war is that 'the boys' have taken the place of the 'young persons'; the flappers can take care of themselves but the poor soldiers—oh Gawd! But these ideas must be kept in mind—cependant, thank God I haven't to meet such people. . . . Hope you're well and taking good care of yourself. I suppose Hindhead will be cold compared to the South, or West I suppose Cornwall is. I'm well fed and fit in a stupid sort of way—unsettled on account of having decided to go to Glasgow . . . So you don't think you'll do this American tour with S. I daresay you're better at home. I can't quite follow him, what about Mrs. S? Well yes, it's a great thing that you've got this chance and are free to make the most of it on your own hook.

Cheer-oh! Gosse—when I said this to Jean she said, 'Away! uncheering oh!' Do I look down hearted?

JDF

In 1917 the first Summer School was held at Combe Martin. I don't think we made any money, but we covered expenses. My mother did the housekeeping and some of the cooking and everyone seemed to enjoy themselves, though the weather was not very good. Fergus went to Scotland and wrote to me from there.

Fergus always spoke of the architect Charles Rennie Mackintosh with the greatest respect and admiration. He had met him with his wife Margaret and Jessie King, in the early days—but had not seen a great deal of them, as Fergus had settled in Paris in 1905. It was not till Toshie decided to give up architecture and devote himself to painting and settled in London about 1915 that he and Fergus became great friends. Toshie and Margaret found a studio at the bottom of Glebe Place. Of course I made them honorary members of my Club and they came to all my performances.

At about this time Katherine Mansfield and Middleton Murry came to London—previously, she had written to Fergus from France:

My official name and address. Madame Bowden,
Hotel Beau Rivage,
Boudre
(Var)

15.1.1918

Dear Fergusson,

Take the word of a 'sincere well wisher' and never attempt this journey during the War. When Murry and I came down here two years ago it was nothing of an ordeal, but this time . . . Well, a hundred Bill Nobles crying Jesus Christ isn't your sofa pillows would not be enough. I would not do it again for all the oranges and lemons and lovely girls dans tout ce pays. I would say: "No! Leave me on the dear old Fulham Road, let me hail the 'bus that none stop, go to the butcher who hasn't any meat, and get home to find the fire is out and that the milkman hasn't come and doesn't intend coming . . ."

Just to mention one or two details. The train was not heated. There was no restaurant car. The windows of the corridor were broken and the floor was like a creek with melted snow. The cabinets did not open. There were no pillows for hire. We were hours late.

The French do not suffer as we do on these occasions. For one thing I think they obtain great relief by the continual expression of their feelings, by moaning, groaning, lashing themselves into their rugs, quietening their stomachs with various fluids out of bottles, and charming the long hours away with recitations of various internal diseases from which they and their friends have suffered . . .

We arrived at Marseilles to find no porters, of course. I was just staggering out when a pimp in white canvas shoes bent on reserving a place for a super pimp bounced up and gave me a blow on the chest which is still a very fine flat ripolion purple. "This, thought I, is Johnnie's Marseilles". And it was the harmonising motif of my stay there. You know the kind of thing. Waiting in a Q for one hour for a ticket and then being told I must have my passport viséd first, and finding myself, after that at the end of the tail again, without even the excuse of the little woman in front of me who got on famously by tapping each man on the shoulder and saying "Pardon Monsieur j'attends un Bébé". Even her ticket seemed to be punched ten times faster in consequence & the porter simply whisked her luggage away. It's quite an idea pour la prochaine fois.

When I did pass the barriers it was to discover that the train for Dandre was due to arrive at all four platforms and there was a terrific crowd on each. Every time a train came in it was thronged by people and even then not an official knew whether it was the right one or not. After two hours of this the real train did arrive, on the furthest platform of course. You picture me running on the railway lines with my rugs, suit case, umbrella, muff, handbag, etc. & finally chucking them and myself into a 1ere where I sat for the next ten minutes in a corner saying to muff "Fool! do not cry. You can't begin crying like a baby at this stage". However, there was suddenly an immense uproar and a body of soldiers rushed the train, commandeered it & began throwing out the civilians bag and baggage. They were not at all a "I-tiddley-i-ty take me back to Blighty" crowd either. They were bad tempered and very ugly. Happily I was in a carriage with 8 Serbian officers and they put up a fight. It was very unpleasant —the soldiers swarming at the windows, tugging at the doors —and threatening to throw you out. But these good chaps lashed the doors up with leather straps, pinned the curtains together and barricaded the door into the passage. They won, and I got here in the middle of the night, walked into a dark, smoky, wet feeling hell, saw a strange woman come forward wiping her lips with a serviette and realised in a flash that the hotel had changed hands. If you will just add to all this 1 raging chill and fever which I caught on the journey I think you will agree that it's not a bad total . . . That was on Thursday.

Today is Tuesday. I have not even unpacked yet—it is cold. Wood costs 2.50 le panier and this hotel is much more expensive. But I shall have to stay here until I am well. At present I spend my time getting in and out of bed—and although there is a bud or two outside the windows & a lilac coloured sea I feel what the charwomen call "very low." At night especially, my thoughts go by with black plumes on their heads and silver tassels on their tails and I sit up making up my mind not to look at my watch again for at least five minutes. However all this will pass or it will pass. To Hell with it.

I thought last night it is a bad thing, during this war to be apart from the one or two people who do count in one's life. After all we are not solitary palm trees in deserts—thank God

—we are groups of two or three with a spring of sweet water between us and a piece of grassy shade.

At this time, to go away alone to another country is a thoroughly bad idea. (This of course is the precisely useful moment for me to make this discovery).

Are you working? You know quite well that I thought of those pictures, don't you. I knew, in a way they would be like that but that did not make them any less of a revelation. They are unforgettable.

Write me a card when you feel inclined to just to give me a hail from your ship.

> Goodbye for now.
> Yours ever
> Mansfield.

Thursday
My dear Fergusson,

Dont cry déja! at the sight of my handwriting and don't be afraid that I shall keep on knocking at your door in this importunate way. I wont.

Only—I can't let my last letter to you remain unanswered, on my side. Make a curl paper of it or use it 'to stop a hole to keep the wind away'. Thanks for yours.

This is an extraordinary country, very well described by an old type I saw today who was picking yellow and white jonquils in his proprieté—I remarked that it was winter before yesterday—"Eh ben—que ce que vous voulez—c'est le façon de not' pays. En jour nous sommes en plein hiver—lendemaing on voyait les boutons et—puis—toute a la fois" and he raised up and stretched out his arms over the flowery field. That is just what has happened. The day before yesterday this whole place, swaddled up to the eyebrows, was rocking, tossing in the arms of the coldest, most biting, unsympathetic nurse you could imagine—But yesterday there came a dawn when the sky and the sea were like silk —and the miracle happened—the sun came out. Toute à la fois the women who had looked like lean boiled fowls became beautiful and fat and rosy. Windows and doors flew open and the houses began to breathe and move. Cats, en escargot, appeared on the window sills. Girls appeared in the doorways plaiting wreaths of yellow immortelles, + every green and blue pitcher went off to the fountain. Old hags in black pleated dresses, with broad black hats tied under the chin with a linen band hobbled in from the country with a load of jonquils on their backs or a pack of olive twigs, and old men swung off into the country, each with a pot of manure on a creaking barrow. There was simply one word that flew over the place like a flag—BEAU. I' fait beau. I' fait ben beau. I'fait vraiment beau."

I went for a walk in the afternoon round by the sea coast. My God, Fergusson, to feel the sun again on ones breast and belly, to realise again that one had five toes on each foot and each toe has a separate voice with which to praise the Lord, and to know that the cheek that was turned to the sea burned as it used to when you were a Kid! Then I turned inland. The lanes are bordered thick with wild candytuft and small marigolds; the almond trees are half in bud half in bloom. All along the way there are little handfuls of earth thrown up, like handfuls of coffee, where the ants are busy. And everywhere you could hear the people working in the fields—you could see them digging on those flat terraces—bending down and raising up again, ample and leisurely, as though they were the children of this kingdom and so had nothing to fear. It was nearing sunset as I came home and each round bright flower was turned to the sun—a cup of light—a sun of its own, and all the olive trees seemed to be hung with bright sparkles. Yes, this is a good place to be in—one word more + then you can throw me out of the window. Heres another thing that struck me as so 'typical' of these people. As I walked back along the main street I saw an old woman on the sea front. She was sitting on a little iron chair which she had planted there, about one inch from the deep sea water. And there she sat—with her back towards the sea doing a bit of crochet. This struck me mildly as "most unwise" as my sister would say, as, had she coughed, sneezed, or taken a false stitch,

over she would have to go. However, it was no affair of mine.
But another old 'un who was washing outside her door
caught side of this. Down fell the wet clothes. 'Marthe' she
shrieked. "Que?" said a voice. "V'en vite" and when Marthe
saw she began to laugh and clap her hands. The windows
became full of heads. "Allez allez! Tu as vu Ma'am Gamel—
la bas? Ah, mon Dieu tu as vu ça?" They came running to
the doors to laugh more and all this time old Ma'am Gamel,
who must have been stone deaf, sat on, doing her crochet,
paying no attention at all.

"Allez allez! elle va tomber."

"Non elle ne tombe pas!"

"Si! elle tombe!"

"Ah si j'avais un orange maintenant par example!"

Every one of them was simply longing to see the Comble
—to see la vieille topple over—I could hear their laughter if
she did—and I can imagine the way they would have leaned
against one another, quite helpless, pointing to her old black
hat & little bit of crochet floating out to sea!

Well, I'll stop. I have a vase of roses and buds before me
on the table. I had a good look at them last night and your
rose picture was vivid before me—I saw it in every curve of
these beauties—the blouse like a great petal, the round
brooch, the rings of hair like shavings of light, I thought
how supremely you had 'brought it off.'

This hotel is quite deserted. I have a room at the end of a
huge, dark, greenish, sous marin corridor which might be
miles away from anybody. I have begun to work—yesterday
—and shall keep at it all I know . . .

I wish I could send you steaks and butter and la richesse de
la terre—But its no go.

Theres nobody to speak to here. Just occasionally I have a
word or two with the lad or with you—but that ends it.
And its quite enough.

> Heres to Art—God bless us all.
> Mansfield.

Look here—don't even like to write.

They took a flat in Redcliffe Road just opposite to the one Fergus had. Mansfield also took a studio in Church Street, Chelsea, almost opposite the Chelsea Art Club—it was a converted garage, not very comfortable, but she said she must have somewhere quite her own where she could write.

All the time they were in Redcliffe Road, Fergus dined with them once a week. They never asked me, but I understood and did not resent this. They wanted to re-live those wonderful years in Paris before the war when they started Rhythm, and which, alas, I had no part in. Mansfield and Murry came to my Club performances and discussions, and Mansfield asked me several times to her studio, but I was always rather afraid of her. I felt immature and inadequate— she already had a reputation as a writer and I knew from Fergus how much she had suffered and still did, both emotionally and physically. But though she talked very freely to me, she never confided in me, so we never became really close friends.

In 1918, Fergus was just within the calling up age and had to go for a medical examination. He was graded A.1. and his friends congratulated him, but he was not so pleased, as he was having a show at Connell's Gallery, Bond Street, in March. He told his friend Konody who was well known in the art world as a writer about it. He said the solution was for Fergus to become a war artist, and got him a personal interview with a colonel at the War Office. I am sorry I have no recollection of his name, because he must have been an exceptional man with a great sense of humour. Konody had provided all information about Fergus's history and his forthcoming exhibition in Bond Street, but when the colonel said he understood Fergus would like to be a war artist, Fergus hesitated, saying that the one thing which worried him was his dislike of the khaki colour of the uniforms! The colonel said, quite seriously, "I'm afraid we can't alter that, but what about the Navy?" Fergus replied that blue was his favourite colour and he had sailed boats all his life so would like nothing better than to do paintings of the shipyards and battleships. The colonel said he would arrange it and they parted on the best of terms.

In July Fergus was due to go to Portsmouth as a war artist and we held our 1918 Summer School again at Combe Martin. I received the following four letters from him:

26th July, 1918. London.
Dear Gosse . . .
I went yesterday and arranged to go to Portsmouth on Monday.

It's all arranged and they've already been told by telephone to expect me, so that's fixed and I'm bound to be there on the 1st or 2nd. Write to Poste Restante.

See that everyone is careful about the bathing and the rocks. I'll hear all the special news when I see you and may be too busy from now on to write much, so don't expect letters.

Now I must go away to the Bank—yes, got the cheque and it's only about two o'clock.

27th July, 1918. London.
Dear Gosse . . . I have everything looked out and ready to put in my bag—and all this evening and the morning to pack. The train isn't till 11.10. Postponing it till Monday has made it all quite easy. Everything is in order, I've even got my ticket, an indiarubber bath and an Ingersoll watch. I arrive in Portsmouth on Monday at 2.11 or about that, and will send an address as soon as possible . . .

30th July, 1918. Portsmouth.
Dear Gosse, I just got your letter at the main Post Office. That part of the town is pretty terrible. This part is quite good and I went down to Southsea last night, it was quite

Eastra With Fruit, 1929, Margaret Morris Collection

wonderful—really like the south of France. The weather is
absolutely amazing, couldn't be finer. The hotel is quite good
and the food excellent, so things are not so bad. I go round
the docks with the Commander man again today. We went
round in a boat yesterday and it was very fine indeed to paint,
but takes a bit of time to select, of course. It was rather a
large order just after an hour and a half queue at the station
and about 4 hours journey, and nothing to eat since light in
the morning, but I'm rested now and will feel more up to it.

I had a letter, just as I was leaving, from Fisher, saying he was moving his boat and would like me to give him a hand, as there's room for three—but I have enough to do . . . I'd like to have a lash at the swimming. I hope to—

Cheer-ho JDF

1st August, 1918. Portsmouth.
. . . everything is going well with me. I went round and saw everything and fixed on several splendid things—one in particular—and it's arranged that I start work at once, so my anxiety is over. The man who has been taking me round is a very nice chap, most intelligent and a great help. He has arranged everything for me but there are a few formalities to be concluded—they will be, tomorrow, so that's all right.

I'll be glad to see you on the 7th or when you like, but let me know well before hand—I may have to state days when I want to do things. I'm very well and at ease now and can enjoy the good news about M—very good indeed. Yes, it is most tantalizing, the country is difficult—don't shout, etc. I'm glad you're getting at the painting—you could paint things in and paint them out—still, drawings are better, smaller, and paints are dear.

Cheer-ho JDF

I got back to London in August and was determined to go to Portsmouth to see Fergus—which I did. It was rather frustrating, we rode on buses and ate at restaurants, but I had a room booked at his hotel so the night was wonderful. He was in great form.

17th August, 1918. Portsmouth.
Dear Gosse, I've just sent off your parcels and the 12 o'clock post has arrived and there's no news from you, so I hope you've arrived all right. I've seen the photographs in the Daily Sketch and they're very good, well composed. Yesterday I worked all day till dinner time and had a good

day. Hope you get the parcels, specially the green canvas. The visit was a complete success, if you have got back all right. There's the gong for lunch. See that you send for some of the Sketches.

Cheer-ho JDF

Having returned to Combe Martin for the end of the Summer School, I got Fergus's letter, scribbled in pencil, when he arrived back in London.

Tuesday, 20th August, 1918. London.
Dear Gosse,

I arrived here at 1 o'clock today. Had a very good journey and got a taxi. Expected tremendous trouble with my luggage, being no buses, I thought I wouldn't be able to get a taxi—found everything all right.

Mrs. Hay is away, so I have the house to myself—pity can't take advantage of it. Had a letter from S, she says she's coming here in a fortnight but I'm not keen. Yes, teaching is a nuisance—but it is safe. Good luck.

I read in the train about the accident and it was odd it being at your place. I hope it was none of your people, though I'm glad to hear it's all right. I didn't know if these people were attached to you.

The walk on the hills sounds to me most restful—like being back in my place, free from people . . . still, the trip was a great success—no accidents is the important thing. I'm very well and the weather here is splendid, but it wasn't when I left this morning. There, it seemed to have come to an end and was boring. This is just a note to catch the 5 o'clock post. I'll write in the morning if I have anything to say. Ask M to let me know if she'll come to tea with me some day—say about 3.30. I haven't her address and I'm better not to write anyway.

Good luck, cheer-ho   JDF

After the war there were dozens of empty houses in and around Cromwell Road. Queen's Gate Gardens, a beautiful Square, had several and we inspected one of them. Each floor had a large room that would have made a wonderful studio and Fergus approached the owners, offering to buy the house if permission could be obtained to convert it into flats for artists (he knew people who would put up the money as a speculation). But the authorities turned the suggestion down flat. Today all these big houses are converted into flats, hotels or business premises.

Toshie had another idea about this time—to build a block of modern artists' studios, as so many artists wanted them. They could be sold or let in advance and a suitable site was available, running from the bottom of Glebe Place with a frontage on Oakley Street. He did beautiful designs of simple masses with elegant lines, but they had to be submitted to the London County Council—which turned them down flat, saying they looked like a factory and they could only pass them if he added a few Greek Columns, or swags of fruit or flowers, which of course he refused to do. So the studios were never built.

Toshie also spent much time designing a theatre for me, but alas I had no hope of getting it built so that idea was even less practical than the studios. He gave it up, and concentrated on his painting, going in the summer to Port Vendres, on the French side of the Pyrenees.

I think it was Eugene Goossens who brought George Davison to my little theatre. George Davison was a very remarkable man. He had launched the whole Kodak business in England and was very well off when it came to him that the social life they led—all the money spent on entertaining mostly uninteresting people—was an utter waste of time, and he turned Communist. But he was what a Communist *should be*. He wanted to use what he had to make as many people who were trying to do something, happy and useful. Quite naturally, his wife who had married him as a conventional, successful businessman, did not take kindly to having the gardener asked into dinner etc., so they separated and she divorced him.

George Davison decided the best way to use his money, would be to adopt unwanted children and give them a good start in life. Through Kodak he had become friendly with a leading photographer of the time, Malcolm Arbuthnot, who recommended an ex-secretary of his who was keen on education to look after the adopted children. She was an attractive and very capable young woman called Joan. I met G.D. (as everyone called him) and Joan, after a performance at my little theatre. They were both enchanted with the freedom of movement, and when I told them of our Summer Schools in Devon, G.D. said, "But why not come to Harlech?" He offered the use of his grounds and a large hall free, so the next Summer School in 1919 was at Harlech.

Fergus and I got very friendly with G.D. He had a large house in Holland Park and said we must stay with him during the Summer School. He had built a house at Harlech called 'Wernfaur', with a large hall and under this hall a flat. He suggested that we and the Goossens could share the flat, but have our meals with him, which we did.

G.D. was a wonderful host. Although he was on a strict diet, he provided whatever his guests wanted to eat or drink. The talk was always interesting and stimulating. Fergus got very friendly with the gardener, Holt, and told him he would like to try his hand at sculpture, as his forbears were masons and joiners. One day Holt, with the help of several other gardeners, brought down a large block of pink granite he had found on the hill above Wernfaur. Fergus was delighted, and at once started work to create three heads, G.D., me and himself. He got chisels from the blacksmith, but broke

them over and over again. He had not realised that this lump of stone had been weathering probably for generations. Eventually he conquered it, and of course gave G.D. the sculpture, which he was delighted with. A then famous American photographer, Alvin Coburn, was staying with G.D. and he took photographs of it, getting us to pose above the sculpture for one of them.

The evenings were great fun. G.D. loved discussions, a free for all and no chairman which became a bit chaotic at times. He sent invitations to the miners who camped in part of his grounds and to the visitors at the Harlech Golf Hotel. These strolled in, usually late and in evening dress—we called them the waiters brigade—but a good time was had by all and really interesting discussions sometimes developed. There were many musical evenings. G.D. had a huge electric organ in the big hall, which he loved to play and did very well. Then, Eugene Goossens and Arnold Bax would play their compositions and sometimes improvise. I remember one amusing evening just for G.D.'s friends and my Summer School. We did a cod opera—I was the prima-donna, Boonie, tall and handsome (but very well covered!) was the prima ballerina. A Spaniard, a musician but not a singer, called Pedro de Morales, was the hero and Goossens and Bax improvised the music. It was great fun. Fergus would not take part but enjoyed it tremendously.

G.D. made everything as perfect as possible, but he could not control the weather which was very bad—torrents of rain with occasional flashes of brilliant sunshine. Posing for photographs on the beach was *hell!* . . . waiting for the sun to come out in a cold wind, wrapped in blankets. But it did us no harm and we got many good pictures. We were all sad when the Summer School was over and we had to return to London.

Fergus had made many sketches and was longing to settle down to painting, so it was a shock to find his landlady in Radcliffe Road was giving up the house and he would have to find another studio. When G.D. heard of this he at once offered Fergus a room in his house in Holland Park. This Fergus was very glad to accept, and moved with his kit bag, having warehoused his furniture. Meantime I had acquired a first floor flat at 15 Callow Street, off the Fulham Road. I still lived with my mother and aunt, but I knew I must have somewhere away from 'home' and 'school', to have a life of my own. Of course I wanted Fergus to move in there, but he was afraid for my reputation—so, he put in his easel and painting table and did many important paintings there, but went to sleep at G.D.'s in Holland Park.

In 1920 I thought I would try a Summer School in France and took 'Le Château des Deux Rives', a large house on a cliff, a promontory running into the sea, with a large garden and lovely views. Perfect, except for the weather which was no better than Harlech! Almost constant rain, but there were large rooms and plenty to do in Dinard: tea-shop, cinemas and the casino. Jo Davidson and his wife Yvonne came, so I got Fergus to come too and we all had a great time.

G.D. begged me to have another Summer School at Harlech. He enjoyed the activity and his nine adopted children loved the classes, so I did. The Goossens, Fergus and I returned in 1921. I don't remember the other guests, except Arnold Bax again, and Harriet Cohen, the pianist.

The gardener, Holt, who had brought Fergus the stone for the three heads, brought him a piece of oak, saying why not try wood instead of stone? So Fergus carved a figure, following the curve of the wood, and called it *Oak Rythm*. It was bought by the Tate Gallery in, I think, 1963. For Fergus, the outstanding feature of the second Summer School at Harlech was the goats that G.D. had recently acquired. They were mountain goats, used to living and breeding among rocky crags, so G.D.'s estate suited them perfectly. They jumped from rock to rock completely sure-footed. What fascinated Fergus was the way their hair grew. I am told they must have been Angoras, it was long but stood out in frills round their legs, like trousers. Fergus made endless drawings of them, but said they must be done as sculpture, so when back in London he got a lump of plasticine and beat it into a solid block, then he carved it into a goat he called *Trousers*, and got it cast in brass. Later he had it enlarged for exhibition and I am now selling the large goat in a limited edition.

One day we had the luck to come on one of these goats who had just produced a kid. It was all wet and staggered to raise itself onto its four little black hoofs. Fergus said, "Isn't that wonderful, they're born with their boots on!"

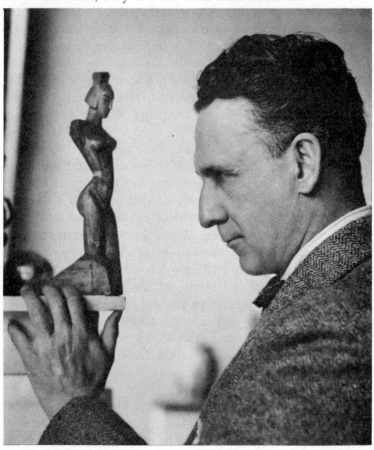

By this time G.D. had a baby daughter by Joan. She was premature. When I first saw her in an incubator in London, her face was no bigger than a doll's. She was now nearly two, a very beautiful child, but fragile and delicate, and G.D. was worried because the doctor said he did not think she could stand another cold, damp, Welsh winter. Fergus advised taking her to the south of France for the winter where, strangely enough, G.D. had never been. Fergus assured him the sun shone most days, and if sheltered from the wind off the Alps, one could sit and eat out of doors all the time. G.D. took his advice and booked a suite at the Grand Hotel, Juan-les-Pins. There was hardly anyone there; the Casino was closed. There was an empty house next to it, the 'Villa Gotte' which had a garden with palm trees opening onto the beach. G.D. just bought it—I am sure at a very low price, for no one came to Juan-les-Pins, even in winter. He wrote to Fergus that the sun did always shine and he would not go back to England. He would sell 'Wernfaur', and have all his furniture and his electric organ sent to the south of France. He furnished just the rooms he needed in the 'Villa Gotte' very simply, got adequate heating and plenty of service, as everyone was unemployed. When they were settled in, he wrote saying we must come and spend Christmas with them.

Our room opened onto the garden with palm trees and the beach beyond and the sound of the sea. Doreen was a different child, loving the garden and the beach and gaining in strength and beauty all the time. Christmas dinner was on the terrace in blazing sun. G.D. was determined to settle here, but he wanted a property with a sea frontage to make a private bathing place and gardens and woods as well.

Fergus said he knew the very place—on the end of the Cap d'Antibes, facing almost due south. He had cycled round the Cap so often and noticed this long, stone building—a shell with trees growing inside it. He had learned that it had been started about sixty years ago by King Leopold of the Belgians to be a palace for Cleo de Merode. When the walls of the ground floor rooms were completed, he was told he could not add another stone to them, as it would cut out the light from the phare! It swings round the Cap every few seconds. So he abandoned the whole project, and bushes and trees had since grown within the walls. G.D. was enchanted with the place and at once said he would buy it. But he was worried at the great height of these ground floor rooms, as he could not build on to them. I saw at once that the height of the walls was enough to allow for a first floor to be put in at either end, leaving the centre for a high dining room, library and a hall for his electric organ. Of course my plans had to be carried out by a French architect which all took about a year.

Meantime, Fergus had gone back to Scotland as his oldest friend John Ressich had offered to take him on a tour of the Highlands in his car—the only way to see them. Fergus was delighted and joined Ressich in Glasgow, taking sketch books, and some water colours. I have found an itinerary of this trip by John Ressich:

29th May–10th June

Started from Glasgow at 9 o'clock on Tuesday, the 29th of May, passing through Perth at 12.30. Went by Forfar, Brechin and Stonehaven to Aberdeen. In the former towns the chief feature was the area of flat grey caps and in Stonehaven a thick mist. Hunted Old Macher Cathedral churchyard unsuccessfully for the authentic Matheson graveyard. Pushed on to Braemar the same night arriving at 6.30. Saw the Smiths.

We left immediately after lunch on Wednesday for Pitlochry via Glenshee and Kirkmichael. In Pitlochry a hat was bought by Mr. Fergusson. Having got this straightened out we proceeded by Blair Atholl and the commonplace road

through Glengarry to Dalwhinnie where taking the wrong turning we very fortunately made Newtonmore and turned there to come back by Laggan and the Loch Laggan road to Spean Bridge. The road through Loch Laggan was one of the most beautiful of our trip, Ben Alder Forest particularly on the south shores striking our attention. Stayed the night at Spean Bridge.

The weather was still glorious when we left next morning by the Inverness road past Loch Lochy and the south end of Loch Ness to Invermoriston where we turned west and worked our way through Glenmoriston to Glen Shiel, Dornie Ferry reaching the Kyle of Lochalsh towards 6 o'clock. Glenmoriston although not on such a grand scale as some of the other Glens holds one of the most pleasant roads that we struck while Glen Cluanie where we had lunch at the little hotel, and a good lunch too, is situated amongst some of the most wonderful hills we struck. From the turn of Loch Duich to Dornie and again from the other side of the Ferry the road is very precipitous and dangerous.

The Kyle of Lochalsh is too reminiscent of Gourock to dwell on. We went on board 'The Plover' next morning about 5.30 and sailed punctually at 6 o'clock through the Near Sound past Raasay, the north end of Skye for Scalpay Island and Tarbert. The boat drew alongside the pier at both these places and it was interesting to observe the fish-curing workers at Scalpay with their mounds of light wooden casks all ready for the herring harvest. From Tarbert we sailed down the east side of Harris passing the Sound of Harris till we reached Loch Maddie in North Uist.

From the Starboard bow crossing the Minch we saw the Shiant Isles stated recently to have been purchased by Mr. Compton Mackenzie. Our first view of Skye was probably under conditions as perfect as could have been imagined when we saw it the previous evening from the hills above Glen Shiel and this morning when we slipped through the Kyle of Lochalsh the Cuillins standing out blue against a cloudless sky with a north-east wind.

With the exception of Stornoway Loch Maddie seems to be the most important little place in the Hebrides and apparently prosperous. From Loch Maddie we went across to Dunvegan which was our first actual contact with Skye as we went ashore there and walked almost as far as the village. From Dunvegan we sailed down during the evening as far south as Loch Boisdale which we reached about midnight on a perfect night.

Through the night we sailed west for the south end of Skye and Mallaig eventually reaching the Kyle of Lochalsh about 8 o'clock on Saturday morning. It is worth putting on record that the Skipper (Duncan Robertson) and the Chief Mate (Macleod) downwards including both stewards and a man who whistled beautifully in the engine-room, the executive of this little ship were universally polite and capable.

Recovering the car undamaged we started for the Black Isle and were fortunate in striking an intelligent police sergeant who told us to risk the more or less private road through Duncraig by the north shore for Strome Ferry. This was one of the most beautiful roads of our trip and was particularly noticeable for the amazing profusion of whin blossom. At Strome Ferry where the tide was dead out we learned they had not had rain for three months and certainly the aspect of the country seemed to confirm it. Our road took us through comparatively uninteresting hills, especially at Achnashein where we had quite the worst food of our voyage and where I was furiously attacked by an octogenarian serving lady who refused to allow me to use the table water for my car radiator.

Through Strathpeffer and the flat country round Dingwall we rose a bit then turned down on Kessock Ferry where we found our friends. We stayed the night there and left the following day at 12 o'clock through Beaulieu and over the beautiful hill above Drumnadrochit at the head of Glen Urquhart where we again picked up Loch Ness and lunched at the attractive hotel of Invermoristen where the landlord thought he could not remember that there was a decent hotel at Arisaig and we both decided that he would have been better at Alexandria Park marking a book in the silver ring. The weather was still superb—almost too much so and our faces by now were not only burned but blistered.

As we passed again through Fort Augustus and Spean Bridge for Banavie just short of Fort William, despite the sun and the heat Ben Nevis, like so many of the high tops, had a cap of snow. Here as elsewhere the Grampian Power Scheme is in full blast and to use a homely expression 'it is to be hoped that when it is all over they will clean up the mess.'

As far as Glen Finnon which is at the head of Loch Shiel this road is comparatively uninteresting but from that point onwards it is probably one of the worst in Scotland—at any rate it was the worst we experienced. To counterbalance this the scenery is superb if we eliminate Mallaig which is a pure depression and from which discovering fortunately that the only habitable hotel had been burned down we fled at a rate of knots and found sanctuary in Arisaig having been refused admission at Morar which with its Loch and all-round scenery is probably the most beautiful place that we struck on our whole trip. There we spent Sunday night in comfort and on looking out of my bedroom window on Monday morning I was interested to see a fat slob of a Cuckoo being mobbed by a flock of obviously aggrieved spugs who were pecking it vigorously to which its only defence appeared to be making noises like a cheap Swiss clock.

The fine weather was no myth at Arisaig as they were suffering from a shortage of water.

On our return we halted after passing through Glen Finnon and had a look at Prince Charley's monument. From the road, that is to say about a hundred-and-fifty yards away, the monument undoubtedly impresses as it is a good shape and colour and Charley's feet are not seen but a closer inspection entirely dispels the illusion and we were particularly struck, apart from the mess that had been made with the kilt and the legs, that the sculptor intentionally or accidentally had

143

given us a very complete summary of the whole affair by the way he had fixed Charley's elegant left leg in a trailing attitude. On the surrounding wall there are three large cast-iron plates setting forth in Gaelic, English and Latin the reason for the monument and the name of the Macdonald of Glenaladale who erected it. It was depressing but inevitable that the heads of six small figures of armoured men decorating these plates had been broken off as souvenirs.

We passed through Fort William and lunched at the South Ballachulish Ferry Hotel. A very first-class situation and hotel where we were attended to by two elderly bald-headed coots who ought to have been in Simpson's in the Strand. On asking the younger of the two what he could tell me about the hills in Glencoe he backed away from me bleating. 'Hills, sir?' and subsequently, we understand, he locked himself in the lavatory and remained there. A fair lunch only and the most expensive of our trip.

We then proceeded through the abomination of desolation called Ballachulish and its slate quarries. An unattractive mass of building on the hillside facing the west caught our attention and a woman of the district when we asked what it was informed us it had been built or bought, I am sorry to say I cannot recall which, by the late Lord Strathcona and it is interesting to recall that before either of us had time to make any observation she offered the comment that it looked just like an institution, with which one must agree. At the Bridge of Coe just before we tackled the Glen we met what Virgil would call a countryman. I asked him what the roads were like. 'Awful bad' he said with a delighted grin. 'Are the hills bad?' I asked apprehensively. 'Oh aye, they're awfu' bad tae.' 'It's a hell of a prospect' I said to him. 'it is that' he said grinning delightedly. So we left having brightened the day of the only inhabitant we were to see till we past King's House Inn. Just before we reached King's House we noticed a ruined cottage or perhaps cottages railed off in the centre of a little bit of rising ground and we conjectured that this probably was the preservation of the scene of the Massacre.

From the rising ground after we passed King's House we had the most perfect view imaginable. To the north-west lay the Moor of Rannoch. Behind us on every side were the great hills rising green, brown and then disappearing in blue. Pushing on through Tyndrum, Crianlarich, we turned east for Killin and passing through Fortingall we reached the height above Tummel. We were especially struck by the appearance of the Fortingall village and district and learned from a boy that the Lady Bountiful of the district is a daughter of the late Sir Donald Currie who is married to one Moltano. Whether he or she has the taste is immaterial but combined with Donald's money it appears to have made not only an attractive but a prosperous countryside. Having failed to assassinate a peewit cheeper which we left standing giving an imitation of Struba's little man we dropped down a perfect road with a wonderful view of the hills above the Tummel and crossed that river at the Tummel Bridge and reached Loch Rannoch. Guided by what we afterwards discovered was the schoolmaster we decided on the Bunrannoch Hotel and had no regrets even when we left on Tuesday morning just to return a few hours later in tow of Mr. Mackintosh. Mr. Mackintosh having failed to estimate the weight of the two, or probably because his method of progression in a car is more suited to a kangaroo than an anxious human being, left us stranded about a mile outside Kinloch Rannoch and proceeded with Fergus right in to the yard of the garage. On dismounting and missing us he looked under the car, looked all round him, looked suspiciously at Fergus, scratched his whiskers, then said, 'Oh it's all right, I know where they'll be,' and returned for us.

This might indicate the end of the song so far as motoring is concerned but having decided against trains and finding that the parts were not presenting themselves from Coventry as swiftly as we had hoped we decided on Sunday the 10th June to beat it but before leaving Kinloch Rannoch we made a circle of the Loch which worked out at twenty-three miles. Near the westerly end there is a very romantic-looking square tower on a small island just big enough you would say to hold it. We were very exercised with this and imagined all sorts of romantic stories, but learned from a character named Scott who owns a Johnny-a'-things shop at the south end of the little village of Kinloch Rannoch, that it was built only a century or two ago by the Clan Menzies on the occasion of the west end of Loch Rannoch being flooded, in order to preserve their rights to the flooded area. It was during the reign of one of the Menzies family who were notorious for their foolish ostentation that it was used as a wine cellar by the occupants of the 'Big Hoose' and this pleasant and cooling practice was only discontinued on two crofters being rescued, full of the Menzies liquor, weighed down with bottles outside and bottles inside, but determined not to lose their spoil; they were nearly drowned before they got them ashore.

On the south side of the Loch the mansion of Captain Wentworth called Dell House is a piece of Scottish architecture worthy of its setting.

We left Kinloch Rannoch by motor bus to Pitlochry: by motor bus to Perth and by motor bus from there to Cathedral Street where we were rescued by one of a crowd of bystanders and brought out in a taxi. It is perhaps worthwhile noting that this whole journey occupied from 10.15 until 5.30. On the way in the Glasgow bus a person seated himself beside Fergus and quite solemnly asked him if the climate in Australia were better than the climate in Scotland as he was sick of Scotland.

Just south of Perth at the end of the long hill that runs down to the Earn at a place called, I think, Dalreoch, we were held up for a few minutes by a wonderful herd of Ayrshire cows with a sprinkling of Jerseys which came from an extraordinary well designed and built steading at the side of the road.

In 1922 my Summer School was at Pourville near Dieppe, a charming little town still unspoiled, with good bathing and charming country around. Many artists joined us there, among them Lett Haines, Cedric Morris, and an American

poetess, Edna St. Vincent Millay, who read her poems very well. Fergus came for part of the time. Later we joined G.D. and Joan at the 'Villa Gotte' in Juan-les-Pins. There, Fergus did many sketches which later became pictures.

Of course there were many trips to the Cap to see how the building and the clearing of the grounds was getting on. G. D. had decided to call it 'Le Château des Enfants'. Fergus noticed that there were two small hotels quite near, but of course shut for the summer, as was the large Hotel du Cap. He said, "Why not have a Summer School on the Cap d'Antibes?" G.D. thought it a great idea, saying we could hold the classes in his grounds and use his hall for evening events as at Harlech. He would also make a way down to the sea. So we could all bathe there. So I booked the Hotel Beau Site for the summer of 1923.

We hurried back to London from the south most regretfully, but Fergus wanted to start work on the highland landscapes he had done so many sketches for.

There is little to say about the next six months, because Fergus was literally painting every minute he was not sleeping or eating. He never got up very early, but started work around 10 o'clock. He would stop for a plate of porridge with a pint of milk and then paint till the light went. In the Spring he changed to fruit and salad instead of porridge. He got through an amazing amount of work because he just refused to go anywhere or see anybody, even real friends. After his evening meal, he would read a little and then go to bed. He always slept wonderfully right through the night.

Fergus's oldest friend, Ressich, had been working hard on his behalf in Glasgow and Edinburgh, writing articles and seeing dealers. Finally he arranged for his first one-man shows in Scotland, to be in 1923 at the Scottish Gallery, Castle St., Edinburgh, and Annan's Gallery, Charing Cross, Glasgow.

Fergus used for his introduction to the catalogue what he had written in 1905 for his first London exhibition, which he said still held good.

> As it is necessary to understand the artist's intention, in order to estimate his achievement:
> He would explain—
> That he is trying for truth, for reality; through light.
> That to the realist in painting, light is the mystery; for form and colour which are the painter's only means of representing life, exist only on account of light.
> That the only hope of giving the impression of reality is by truthful lighting.
> That the painter having found the beauty of nature, ceases to be interested in the traditional beauty, the beauty of art.
> Art being purely a matter of emotion, sincerity consists in being faithful to one's emotions.
> As no emotion can be exactly repeated, it is hopeless to attempt to represent reality by piecing together different impressions.
> To restrain an emotion is to kill it.
> What may appear to be restraint may be the utmost limit of one's power.
> What may appear to be the utmost limit of one's power may be restraint.
> Brightness is not necessarily meretricious, nor dinginess meritorious.
> It is absurd to suppose that everyone must be slow to understand—some have insight.
> What is on the surface may explain everything to one with real insight.
> That the artist is not attempting to compete with the completeness of the camera, nor with the accuracy of the anatomical diagram.　Genius is insight.

By July 1923 G.D., Joan and Doreen had moved into the 'Château'. They arranged a suite for Fergus and me under theirs, opening onto the patio which had a fountain in the middle. We had a room each with a bathroom between and there was fine wire-netting on all the windows. This was very necessary in those days as mosquitos were very plentiful and often poisonous. Our windows looked on to the woods that led down to the sea; the songs of the birds were wonderful—the nightingales sometimes kept us awake.

G.D. had sent for the gardener Holt, who in Harlech had found the lump of pink granite out of which Fergus carved the three heads, who was busy making a way to get down to the sea. The Cap d'Antibes runs nearly two miles out to the sea. The château woods ran to a bay facing due south, with cliffs of jagged rocks about twelve feet high, and water about fifteen feet deep. Lovely for diving, but no way out. Holt got many bags of cement, and made rough steps and a small platform, from which he got a spring-board fixed with a ladder at the end. All was in order by the time my Summer School started. Classes were in the château grounds in which of course Doreen and the adopted children joined, and everyone bathed off the rocks and afterwards sun-bathed in the woods or on the rocks. When they got too hot, they dived into the sea again.

Fergus got much inspiration, and did hundreds of sketches over the years, from which he painted many pictures. In the water-colours he usually used touches of colour indicating the costumes worn, but in the oils he usually made the figures nude, though he never actually saw them that way.

When we got back to London Fergus had a great painting spell, then in December a letter came from Ressich—

16.12.23. Sunday.
Dear Johnnie,
    The stage is set—a climax reached.
    You would get the 'Herald' following my last two letters. Reid senior, who hitherto has hung back is now definitely

FOR the idea of accepting the three of you as a GROUPE ECOSSAIS (his own christening). The local Press is agog: all-round interest has been created—in short the moment has come—hence my letter in the 'Glasgow Herald'.

Our work is bearing fruit.

Reid senior is back at work full of fight, cursing the Englishman, and more important still—a Paris dealer has just been here staying with him. I may not have got his name quite correctly but it is something like Bignon, 8, rue de la Boetie, which Hunter tells me is THE street now. He saw your stuff and wants to come in too and has I gather definitely offered to give the combined show in the Brabazagne Gallery, after Dundee and Glasgow, some time between April and July. Twenty pictures of each of you—total 60.

Now my 'Herald' letter was also timed to click with the ART CLUB dinner on Friday last at which the new Lord Provost was the guest. Out of malice aforethought, Hunter and I appeared and in the big room before and after the dinner, and in the dining room during the dinner I manoeuvered us into a conspicuous position (The Reds!). As Percy Robb would say, it was great. Everyone was talking about my letter. I was presented to the Lord Provost (a very good type); people including Bone the sailor-author brother, came up and asked to be introduced—splendid—then the Provost's speech when he came to municipal interest in the pictures, the decent man practically said 'yes' to me letter. All the lay members were raising a cheer for it while the 'artists'—the Domes of Silence with their chinchilla moss—nursed their bellyache and muttered and scowled at Hunter and me. Poor old Hunter can hardly keep his feet on the ground.

But it's YOU I'm concerned about. The chance has come and there is only one thing to be done and that is to get that money in, come here and get your selection of your pictures made and cleaned and framed and go right ahead. I can do no more now than keep it going but we've got to deliver the goods.

Lily and I hope to be in London on the 28th, and I shall see you early on Saturday morning.

The opportunity has been created.

Yours

Jock

In 1924, after a busy winter and spring for Fergus, we had the second Summer School at the Cap d'Antibes. In 1923 old Mr. Sella, proprietor of the Hotel du Cap, had asked me to bring my girls to bathe at Eden Roc and he would get photographers and would start a *Summer Season* in the South of France in 1924. He offered me the use of three empty cottages for my teachers and pupils.

Old Mr Sella invited the Comte de Beaumont and his wife, Picasso and his first wife, and Fitzgerald to be his guests to start the Season. I was to give performances on several evenings. Mr Sella advertised these very well and put up raised seating and very good lighting so all performances were well attended. He begged Fergus and myself to come and bathe at Eden Roc, to support his few guests! So we did, though we much preferred the seclusion of the château bathing place.

The first morning we came to the Hotel du Cap, we entered from the back and walked through the Hotel to the wide 'carriage way' leading to the sea. The first person we saw was Picasso. He greeted us saying, 'Ah mon vieux copain Fergusson', and embraced him warmly. Fergus expressed surprise at finding Picasso in this conventional hotel, to which he replied that his wife liked it, but he hated it. He said that when they had (he made a gesture of pulling a chain, saying sushh!) they thought they had the whole of civilisation! "But why are *you* here?" he asked. Fergus explained that we were at the 'Château des Enfants', next door.

Picasso had rented a motor launch and wanted us to go with them to the Islands. Fergus firmly refused, but said I would be delighted to go. So I had to. Picasso's first wife was a ballet dancer and was only interested in the pearls and diamonds Picasso had given her, so my main occupation on these trips to the islands was to *hold her jewels* while she bathed. I felt like throwing them into the sea.

One day we met Picasso at Eden Roc and we walked back to the hotel together. He said, "You do not fit into this place", and he picked a sprig of bog-myrtle from a bush and handed it to Fergus saying, *"This is you."*

Fergus pressed it between heavy books and found his initials in it and he used the design on several catalogues. I still have the sprig and reproduce it here.

Fergus was glad to get back to London because he had a show of his Highland landscapes going on shortly at the Leicester Galleries. In November he got a letter from the Lefèvre Gallery in King Street suggesting a group show in February 1925 if Fergus would gather together the artists. Time was short, but he wrote letters to the artists he felt should take part, saw to printing of posters, etc., and asked P. G. Konody if he would write the foreword to the catalogue.

Charles Rennie Mackintosh and his wife wrote to us from the Pyrenèes about the Leicester Gallery show.

Hotel du Midi,
Ille sur la Tet,
Pyrenees Orientales.   1 Feby, 1925
Dear Ferguson [*sic*[

We had the 'Observer' of 11th January sent to us and we were both greatly interested to see that you were showing your beautiful Scottish pictures at the Leicester Galleries.

It is quite understandable that Walter Sickert should appreciate them so much and I do hope that at last the buying public have come to realize their true artistic value. I have not forgotten the impressions they had on me when we saw them at Chelsea. I still have such a vivid mental picture of them that I can pass them in review one by one making a sort of subconscious 'peep-show' and see them quite clearly just as you showed them to us. This is a most valuable gift I possess as I can see your pictures whenever I like and for as long as I like.

I hope you will write and tell me that the Show was a great financial success and if you have one or two spare catalogues I shall be glad to have these. We are now settled in our beloved Ille sur Tet. There is nobody here but ourselves and we are as happy as sandboys. I wish you and Meg could come here for 3 or 4 months either to work or rest.

This is a splendid little Hotel and we only pay 18 francs (4 shillings) per day. The food is good and plentiful, the people are simple and kind and altogether it is an ideal place as I said for rest or work.

The eating room is a delightful feature. At the end is a long table the full length of the room at which the workmen sit. There are usually 8, 10 or 12 splendid fellows sitting here having a gorgeous feast and discussing the affairs of the world It always somehow reminds me of 'The Last Supper' only there is no frugality here and the wine flows in a way that would have given life and gaiety to 'Leonardo's' popular masterpiece.

We shall be here until the end of May then we go to Mont Louis for 2 months and then back here or perhaps we may go to Montpellier to stay with Professor Pat Geddes for a month or so.

Meantime we shall expect to get a long letter (this is a long letter) telling us what you are both doing and if you could tell us that you were coming here for some months we would be the happiest people in the world.

Love to you both.

Yours always,

C. R. Mackintosh

Dearest Meg,

I am sure you are feeling very happy indeed now that London is acclaiming Fergusson as the great artist the few have always known him to be. It must be very cheering for him too to get such discriminating notices. Write when you have time and tell us all your news.

Best love to you both,

Margaret M.M

Enclosed with the letter was a copy of this poem.

THEN shall thy circling armes embrace and clip
My willing bodie, and thy balmie lip
Bathe me in juyce of kisses, whose perfume
Like a religious incense shall consume,
And send up holy vapours to those powres
That blesse our loves, and crowne our sportfull houres.

No wedlock bonds unwreathe our twisted loves;
We seeke no midnight Arbor, no darke groves
To hide our kisses; there, the hated name
Of husband, wife, lust, modest, chaste, or shame,
Are vaine and empty words, whose very sound
Was never heard in the Elizian ground.

All things are lawfull there, that may delight
Nature, or unrestrained Appetite;
Like, and enjoy, to will, and act, is one,
We only sinne when Loves rites are not done.

THOMAS CAREW (1640)

The Lefèvre show was successful too and many things were sold. Konody's foreword was very good, but he completely ignored Fergus as a sculptor although he had four pieces in the show. He had known and admired Fergus for years, but as a painter. Fergus was over fifty before he started carving. For some time now, there has been as much demand for Fergus's sculpture as for his painting, and sculptures have been bought by the Tate Gallery, the Museum of Modern Art in Edinburgh and the University of Glasgow.

 # PARIS 1925~1939

Fergus felt it was now time to go to Paris again, but he would have to find a studio. 14, Radcliffe Road had been sold and he had warehoused his belongings meantime. So we returned to Paris late in 1925, taking a room in the cheapest hotel we could find, in Montparnasse—the district Fergus knew and loved. It was the Hotel des Académies, in the rue de la Grande Chaumière where the Boulevard Raspail crosses the Boulevard Montparnasse.

We were lucky to get a top room, the cheapest because there was no lift. There was hot and cold water in the room and a comfortable bed. And there were no restrictions about eating in one's room, which we mostly did on fruit, salads, cheese, nuts and *real* wholemeal bread. We were also lucky to have a small Health Food shop quite near—Fergus knew it before the first world war! The same woman was in charge. To ourselves we called her 'the defender' because she always looked so grim and determined and when we asked her how she was, she always replied, "Je me défends!" as if she would attack us. She sold the best bread I have ever tasted. It came in three styles: the first, a very attractive pale brown; the second, called 'integrale', absolutely whole wheat, which we always bought; the third, made with molasses, almost black, good just with butter but too strong a taste with other foods. Fergus looked around for a studio while I did the shopping and made the salads.

It must have been in the summer of 1925 that we met Charlie MacArthur, the American writer who later married Helen Hayes. Someone brought him to bathe at the Château des Enfants from G.D.'s rocks. He was interested in painting and he and Fergus had long discussions. It happened that Mrs Whitney had seen an exhibition of Fergus's pictures and sculptures in London, and offered him a show at her gallery in New York in 1926, so of course Fergus asked MacArthur's advice on whether he ought to make an effort to go to New York for the opening. Charlie looked at him very seriously and finally said "I don't think you would be any help, you don't look to me the type of man who would hold the ladies' hands and send them away all in a glow!" Fergus was very relieved and asked him if he would write a foreword for the catalogue. Eventually he did, and I quote it here:

> Fortunately, John Duncan Fergusson is in Europe, which makes his introduction to America a rather simple matter. There is no telling how it would be accomplished with Fergusson around. He is one of those dour, wind-bitten Scots—at least three parts granite. As well shake hands with Ben Lomond.
>
> Such as Fergusson despise the gab and grimaces so necessary to further acquaintance. I'm sure that he is glowering at these restrained remarks of mine. For he is as blunt and straightforward as his work, and the only person who can tell him anything is a man named Fergusson.
>
> A famous London critic once said of him: 'I know of no living painter with a more profound feeling for the music that is in color. The joy of life and the joy of stating it is everywhere in his work.' Yet Fergusson's work represents a very high boiling point. He is not the one to faint at every sunset. But when he does respond it is thrilling.
>
> This is his first comprehensive American showing. Characteristically, it has been a long time getting here. Fergusson is around fifty-two years old and his exhibitions in Paris,

London and Glasgow have been important events for a long
while now. His recognition is fairly ancient.

There is great talk of integrity nowadays. Here it is.

CHARLES MacARTHUR

The show was quite a success and as a result the sculpture
was invited to Chicago, and the Kraushaar Gallery in New
York offered a show in 1928.

In Paris, meanwhile, cheap studios were not easy to find.
All the new blocks of flats had studios on the top, but having
bathrooms and lifts, rents were out of the question. Only
the rich, mostly Americans and some Germans could afford
them. One advertisement gave a reasonable rent, but said
the studio could only be visited during the lunch hour or
after 6 p.m. Fergus went one lunch time and he was charmed
with the studio, large, light and airy. He said he would return
but the occupier was so insistent that he could only come at
the lunch hour, or after 6 p.m. that Fergus was suspicious.
So we took a walk around there at about 4 o'clock and
found that the building under the studio was a saw-mill.
The constant noise was quite deafening—except at lunchtime
and after six!

The old man who really ran the Hotel des Académies, we
seldom saw anyone else, deserves a special mention. He spent
the entire day cleaning the stairs and bedrooms from top to
bottom, and most efficiently. At night he slept on the floor
wrapped in a rug, behind the door of the tiny office where
the bedroom keys were kept. We hated having to wake him
to get our key. He was always cheerful and pathetically
grateful if we gave him something for a small service, such
as taking a message. We longed to be able to do something
really good for him, but of course we could not, being very
hard up. But we always remembered him and I still do with
admiration and affection.

At this time I longed to stay with Fergus continuously, but had to go to my London School though I had just started one in Paris. I kept a suitcase with the essentials in London and in Paris, so I could travel with no luggage whatever. Fergus too had to move around, going to Scotland where Ressich was working for him all the time and watching over his paintings still up there after the exhibitions. He sent the following telegram in January 1926 addressed to Fergus at the Hotel des Académies:

Glasgow 16 16 12 14h40 Have collected seventy five pounds

There was also the Callow Street first-floor in London where I had put my father's easel when I first took the flat, and where Fergus had been painting and keeping pictures, so time had to be spent there too; but the Hotel des Académies served as our base. Every summer we managed somehow to get to Antibes, arriving covered in smuts having travelled third, and both exhausted, but G.D. and Joan always met us with two cars and whirled us into paradise.

Ressich thought that Fergus should go to New York for his second show in 1928, as this would be quite an important one with sculpture as well as pictures, and the Kraushaar Gallery was well-known. Ressich suggested they make the trip together as he had thought for some time of visiting New York. He explained that a director of the Anchor Line was a great friend of his and could get them reduced fares on the *Transylvania*.

So Fergus agreed and away they went. They had a special introduction to the Captain and the Chief Engineer (who was a Scot of course!). They sat at the Captain's table and had the run of the ship. Fergus enjoyed himself thoroughly, spending much time with the Captain on the bridge and in

the engine rooms, or having long discussions with the Chief Engineer. I wish I could remember some of the stories he recounted.

Also at the Captain's table was a very beautiful American woman. Of course Fergus asked if he might make some sketches of her. She sat just opposite him, leaning on her elbows and looking over the centrepiece of fruit with flowers on either side. She looked wonderful. She agreed, and I think he gave her one of the sketches. Eventually he did an oil painting which he called *Transylvania* and exhibited in London. It was bought by the American original! So I have no idea where it is.

In an interview with the *New York Times* Fergus described his impressions of New York and his feelings about Scotland —three days later, he got a letter from 'The Chief of Clannfhearghuis of Stra-chur' and here are some extracts:

The Explorers Club, New York, U.S.A.
Dear Clansman:—
Your interview in the New York Times of 31 October which was handed to me yesterday, interested me greatly. I am indeed glad to find a Scots Gael doing such excellent work for the honour and glory of our ancient Alba.

You said among other things that the Clannfhearghuis was the oldest and proudest clan of Scotland, a sentiment in which I most heartily agree with you. Our clan name, Clann Fhearghuis, was used by our race many centuries before we adopted MacFergus, or Fergus(s)son as a surname . . .

The Fearghusian race which claims descent from Fearghuis I who reigned 335 B.C. and through him to Fearghuis II, the Great, who reigned in 503 A.D. have always been identified with Argyll. I have the honour (or shall we say the misfortune?) to be the representative of the Fearghusian kings of Dalriada, otherwise known as Argyll, which word comes from Earra-Ghaidheal, Territory of the Gael . . .

If interested in Aviation there is to be a lecture on the subject at the Explorers Club at 8.00 o'clock 9 November which promises to be interesting. We could have dinner at the City Club at No. 55 West 44th Street at 6.00 o'clock preceding the lecture.

Your sincere well-wisher,

Clannfhearghuis of Stra-chur.

Fergus certainly enjoyed his short visit to New York, but he said he could not have stood much more of it. The hospitality was amazing, but the habit of invitations to breakfast (!) he found very trying. He liked the skyscrapers, especially in the evenings as the lights came up, but he never made any sketches. He and Ressich stayed at the Brevoort Hotel, an old-fashioned one, and very comfortable; but constant telephone calls and social appointments are not conducive to artistic creation.

One incident I think is worth recounting because it must be unique in the annals of New York restaurants. One evening Fergus and Ressich were having a quiet meal at a good but not fashionable restaurant. Ressich suggested Fergus should have an ice-cream as they were particularly good in America. He agreed, but when a block of ice-cream that Fergus said was enough for six people was placed in front of him, he exclaimed that it was far too much. The waiter said, "You don't have to eat more than you want, sir". Fergus replied, "But I have to pay for all this?" "Yes, sir." "Then it's mine to take away?" "Yes sir, certainly sir, I will bring you a special container." Ressich must have been rather worried when all eyes were turned on their table! But Fergus was oblivious of the sensation he was creating. The waiter packed and wrapped the ice-cream carefully, handing it with a bow to Fergus, who thanked him warmly,

saying he would enjoy it in about three hours time. I am sure Ressich recompensed the waiter well but he told me he had never felt so embarrassed as when, following Fergus carrying the parcel of ice-cream down the room, a great cheer went up from the whole staff and many of the tables!

That same year, 1928, the Lefèvre Galleries did an important exhibition of Fergus's painting and sculpture, so there was no time to hunt for a studio in Paris and it was not until 1929 that someone told us about the Parc Montsouris, which led to the Cité Universitaire where students of all nationalities lived. We went to see it and found it most attractive, lovely trees and lawns, and a lake with ducks. No studios, but there were flats to let and we found one on a third floor with balconies overlooking the park. Two reception rooms had folding doors between them which, thrown open, made a fine studio. There was a bedroom, bathroom and kitchen at the back, central heating and hot water. Fergus decided to take it.

1929 was the last joyous summer we had with our wonderful, gracious host G.D., for a terrible thing happened —a fire started in the Château woods! Everyone was constantly warned how easily fires started in that dry heat. Even a piece of glass reflecting the sun could do it, so nobody should smoke while walking through the woods. Yet a fire started. Of course garden hoses were turned on and buckets of water passed from hand to hand. Eventually the fire brigade arrived and the fire was stopped, but only *just* before it reached the Château, where Doreen and the other children had been sent. Of course G.D. was in a panic and though he was assured all was well, I don't think he ever really recovered from the shock and anxiety, for he died in December 1930.

I don't know when Fergus's idea of presenting a group of modern Scottish painters in Paris actually took shape, he

had talked about it for years. Eventually, helped by the support of Reid of the Lefèvre Galleries in London, the Georges Petit Gallery in Paris expressed interest in the idea.

At that time Lord Tyrrell was British Ambassador in Paris and I was giving massage and exercises to his daughter. One day I told her of this project and at once she said if we could arrange it she was sure that her father would be delighted to open the exhibition. Naturally this impressed the gallery. Ramsay MacDonald was Prime Minister, so would be the obvious person to write a foreword to the catalogue if he would. An old friend of ours, David Graham Pole, knew MacDonald well, so Fergus asked him to make the approach. The P.M. sent him the following reply:

10 Downing Street, 15th January, 1931.
Major D. Graham Pole, M.P.
My dear Graham Pole,
    Thank you so much for your letters. Someone has already written me about the Paris Exhibition. I think it is the same one, but the letter previously sent has gone to the Foreign Office for observations. Unfortunately I do not know the work of your two friends, so that I cannot speak of it on its merits. If you like to use the following words you can do so—
    'I am very glad to hear of your proposed Exhibition of the Scottish artists in Paris. Scottish art is not known nearly so well as it ought to be except for the high prices which are given for Raeburn portraits. The Scottish temperament however, has produced and is still producing really fine artistic work and is kept alive inspired by modern ideas, which, though not breaking with traditions, are carrying it on in a living way. I hope the Exhibition will have such success as will encourage the promoters.'
                                                        J. Ramsay MacDonald.

From then, all went well, but Fergus had to do all the preliminary work, catalogues, posters etc. The Opening of the show was really a great occasion. All Paris (that is noticed) seemed to be there. Lord Tyrrell made a very good opening speech—stressing the 'Auld Alliance' and the 'Entente Cordiale'.

Among Fergus's pictures was a large group of nudes called *La Déesse de la Rivière* (the Goddess of the River) which he had shown to Reid of the Reid Lefevre galleries in London, who said, "Well you'll never sell *that* picture". It was bought on the opening day of the Paris exhibition by the French State and hung in the Luxembourg, together with a Peploe and a Hunter.

Peploe couldn't believe it and wrote to Fergus:

13 India Street, Edinburgh.
My dear J.D.,
    Heartiest congratulations on your success.
    I think we may fairly congratulate ourselves in the event. If I had been told in 1911, when we were in Paris, that I should have a picture in the Luxembourg, would I have believed it possible?
    . . . Margaret sends her love and best congrats to you. She is not a day older—we're aye the same.
                                      yours ever,
                                            S. J. Peploe.

The following year, in 1932, Fergus decided to look for another studio. The one thing we had not noticed when taking the flat at the Parc Montsouris was the children's playground opposite, from which the noise was *deafening*, even with the windows closed. Also, the walk back from the Dôme in Montparnasse was a long trail. This time he was lucky. At 6, rue Ernest Cresson, near the Lion de Belfort at the top of Boulevard d'Orleans, new blocks of flats were going up with studios at the top. Rents were reasonable because, though there was a good-sized studio, with bedroom, bath and kitchen at the back, there was only a very small one-way lift. You had to walk down seven flights! but when coming in with heavy baskets of provisions, you could take the lift up.

Fergus was very happy and painted a lot in that studio—the last he had in Paris.

Gradually more new buildings went up till they formed a complete square. One day Fergus remarked that there had been no letters for a week and he was expecting some, so I went to the Post Office and found a pile of letters waiting. When I asked why they were not delivered, I was told they were wrongly addressed. It was then explained that since the buildings now formed a square, the address had been changed to 'Square Delormel'. When I said we had not been informed, I was told with a smile—"Une petite faute là!"

I had to return to London and Fergus wrote me saying he had met a most attractive and paintable American girl fashion-artist, who was doing the dress 'collections' for American papers—her name was Roberta Paflin, called 'Bobby'. She sat to him and he did several heads of her in the Luxembourg Gardens. When I returned to Paris we became friends, and met again when I went to America in 1954. Only yesterday, in May 1973, I had a letter from her saying she was coming to Europe this summer and hoped to see me.

A most charming, intelligent woman, Rita John, whom Fergus had met long before me in London, on his way to Paris, suddenly arrived at the Château bathing place when we were there on our annual visit. She was staying with her mother who had a villa at Golf-Juan. As always, G.D. made all our friends welcome and she often came to bathe with us. She had sent her daughter Enid to my Summer School at Cap d'Antibes in 1924 when she was 16 and already a wonderful swimmer.

One day Fergus told Rita he had a letter from Jo Davidson, begging us to go to stay with him in the Touraine on our way back to Paris, but it was too difficult to arrange the journey. Rita at once suggested she drive us there. She had known Jo well in London and would love to see him again! So it was arranged and we had a most delightful journey avoiding the main routes. We stopped a night on the way. We had a wonderful reception when eventually we arrived at the Manoir de Bécheron, at Saché near Tours. It was a charming old house built round a square courtyard, only one storey high. Jo and his second wife gave us the warmest welcome—a lovely dinner with wine from their own vineyards! Jo said it cost him a shilling a bottle, but as it would not travel he was glad of help in drinking it. Yvonne had died some years before, and Jo later met Florence Lucius in St. Paul where she was living. She was a painter and Fergus and I were both very fond of her. She was wonderful at looking after Jo, which was not easy by that time for he was far from well. He was still full of the joy of life however, and resented restrictions on food and drink, but he and Fergus had a great time re-living the past and planning the future.

We were all sad when this happy time came to an end, Rita returning alone to Golf-Juan and Fergus and I to Paris, then London, and Fergus to Scotland where he was having a show at the Pearson and Westergard's Gallery in October 1934. But he soon returned to London and on to Paris, as he had many sketches from the south he wanted to paint.

The following summer we managed as usual to get to the south. We put our good health down to the sun, the sea and the many years of G.D.'s hospitality. Besides all he had given us at the Château, he had taken us trips into the hills behind the Riviera, to the Gorge du Loup, etc. and eventually, when he bought a house at Thorenc, we stayed there too while Fergus made sketches for some of his best paintings. These were later done in the Paris studio. The concierge there was most sympathetic. When I was away, unless Fergus had told her he was expecting someone, she only let attractive females up! I was torn in two, having one foot in London and one in Paris, where my school was doing well. Suzanne Lenglen had

adopted my exercises as a basic training in her tennis school, and in London my school had moved to a large house at 31 Cromwell Road through the voluntary help and organization of Lady Norton.

Fergus must have come to London in 1936, because I have the catalogue of an important exhibition at the Lefèvre Galleries held in February, which included oil paintings and sculpture, and another at Barbizon House in November of watercolours.

By June 1937 Fergus must have been painting in Paris and also being preoccupied with the Groupe d'Artistes Anglo-Américains, about which he wrote the following letter:

21st April, 1937.
John Mallet Esq.
Dear Sir,
   I am writing as president of le Groupe d'Artistes Anglo-Américains and for the British members of it, to ask if we can say that our coming show is under the patronage of the Ambassador, and if he will come to the vernissage on the 1st June, 1937. Mr. Kames said he'd speak to you about it and here is the catalogue of our exhibition.

Yours sincerely,
J.D.F

The exhibition took place in the Schola Cantorum, a former monastery belonging to the English Benedictines in the rue St. Jacques. Next, I have a note written in July of that year, from Jo Davidson:

7 rue Cels, Paris XLVe.   2/7/37.
Dear Johnny,
   If I don't see you tonight here is the order to collect my bust and the letter advising them that I have written the dealers that the bust will be called for.
   It was good of you to do that for me, as I think they will

be able to dispose of it for me.

I am rushed to death trying to get away—am leaving Wednesday morning at 6 A.M. arriving Budapest at 2.30 in the afternoon.

I'll be back in about six weeks and we'll celebrate

affectionately Jo

Love to Meg.

The next letter is from another very old friend:

Southpark Avenue, Glasgow, W.2
18th Oct. 1937
Dear Fergusson

. . . Regarding the Glasgow show . . . what about Annan's? I do think you should aim for a show somewhere in Glasgow next year—Exhibition Year (1938 Empire Exhibition)— there's bound to be a huge influx of visitors, surely among them some intelligent collectors. The Exhibition itself, of course, is out to give a boost to Scottish art . . . when I learn anything definite on this point I'll let you know . . .

All the best,

Yours sincerely, Eric de Banzie.

In November came news from St. Tropez where 'Mackay and Melville', as they were always called, had retreated for the winter. Old friends of ours, Agnes Mackay is a poet and Marian Melville an historian and writer—both remarkable women, who lived (and still live) in Paris. Marian is the daughter of Arthur Melville, whom Fergus always acknowledged as a big influence in his painting life. Here is her cousin's letter:

St. Tropez (Nougat Blanc).   2nd November, 1937.
Dear Fergusson,

. . . I do hope you and Margaret are both well and that your work is going well, also the Celtic League, and basic Gaelic—I should love to have news of it all—for I feel real sympathy with all that concerns you and Margaret—and ideas are bread and wine.

God! it is marvellous here in the Autumn—I have never seen such colour—the valleys with the wine red vines beneath the sombre-browed hills—it has all the colour of the heathered glens with something mellow and kind, ancient and classical added. The grey cloud of olive trees and this pure light—it is much more paintable than in full Summer; one can see the colours more.

'Je me retrouve', I feel a sort of beatific happiness: peace —a state of grace which one loses so quickly in town. I become a poet here. Melville loves it too—if we could find a small place we would live here most of the time. Now that all the Parisians have gone home the port resumes its local life. We are staying at Hotel Sube on the port, as our little hotel on the plage has gone to bed for the winter. The harbour is marvellous in the morning light, with sails out to dry and the tartanes lying asleep, it is worth putting up with sounds at night to wake looking out on it.

I feel I should be sending you some nougat wrapped in this paper instead of a letter. By the way, do you like it—the nougat, I mean. I believe it is rather famous, but I am not one of those who dare eat it!

We take our lunch with us and spend most days wandering through the hills as long as it is light. I think poems are founded on 'choses vues' as much as painting—the idea and emotion—no matter how abstract—springs from contemplation of some aspect of beauty—that is, something that moves one (which is perhaps the only acceptable definition of beauty).

I must stop—for you will never be bothered reading even as far as this. If rather 'decousu', please forgive it as I am writing in a small café where country people are playing cards, dogs are excited about cats and there is a genial atmosphere and hum. Melville sends her love, we often talk of you and all your kindness to us in Paris.

Our love to Margaret too—Yours ever, Mackay.

When summer came round again, Jo Davidson persuaded
Fergus to leave earlier for the south and go to Tours where
he would meet us and take us to Bécheron for a longer stay.
We did this and had a wonderful time. Fergus sketched the
house and round about it, making some important pictures
of the subjects later. When Jo took us to see the nearby
Château of Azay-le-Rideau Fergus told me to sketch the
stables with the moat running under an arched bridge, which

we agreed was much more interesting than the château.
Eventually I made a painting of that sketch.

Jo had a wireless and Fergus listened to the depressing news
bulletins with him. This cast a cloud but we continued on
our way south to complete the summer.

Betty Simpson, my second in command, had gone on a
visit to Kitty Macleod, a wonderful Gaelic singer from the
Isle of Lewis, who had come to sing for me at the old Queen's
Hall where we gave a 'Celts and Scots' night. It was one of
the last events there. I improvised to Kitty's singing. Betty
sent Fergus the following letter:

Written on the train to—Port of Ness, Isle of Lewis.
August 14th, 1938.
My dear Fergus—

I am just going through your country and feel I must write
to you. It is a perfectly marvellous day, brilliant sunshine, but
enough white clouds about to make the mountains change
every few minutes from pale blue to indigo. The heather is
out, and I am seeing this part of Scotland for the first time
in really good weather. Today being Sunday there is no boat
to Lewis, so I shall spend the night at Mallaig, and tomorrow
morning if I can get a p. card I'll send you one. This
country is so wonderful that I wonder why on earth so many
Scots live out of it. Why live anywhere else? I shall find it
exceedingly difficult I feel to leave the place once I get there,
and if Barrie was speaking the truth, when he wrote of Mary
Rose disappearing on an island, I should be sorely tempted
to find the same island and disappear! . . .

We are now passing Loch Treig, I have a map with me
and am enjoying following the route . . .
August 15th, Monday morning.

Since I last wrote everything was more and more beautiful,
working up to the climax of a perfect sunset over Mallaig. I
arrived about 4.15 and was thrilled with the place. All the
islands were on view as there was no mist, just most heavenly

blue everywhere and green, and sparkling light. I was staying
at the Marine Station Hotel. Delightful little place, very
clean, with wooden walls inside. Excellent food and comfortable bed, you probably know it. I had a super tea on
arrival, home-made scones, brown bread, home-made jam
and cream with the tea. After tea I changed into some
comfortable clothes, bare legs and sandals and walked along
the road to the Isles, until about 3 miles after Mallaig it seems
to peter out. I made three quick drawings on the way and
nearly went loopy over the beauty of it—the sea was every
bit as blue as the bluest day at Antibes, and the rocks were
white and pale grey, with tufts of magenta heather and
yellow flowers . . .

So much love to you

from Betty

I also had a letter from Betty, which sadly I cannot find,
in which she described bathing with the seals and how
friendly they were. They would come all round her. She
sometimes managed to climb on one of their backs, then the
seal would dive down to dislodge her and come up to blow
water in her face! Then she would dive down and blow water
in his face. When she took a long swim they did not follow
her, but when she got back they all gathered round again
for more fun and games. Betty did not mind cold water and
bathed happily in mountain streams and waterfalls.

When we got back to Paris from the south, we found the
tension in the air more acute. Fergus decided to give notice
at his studio and pack up his pictures and belongings. This
was completed before going to Antibes the next summer—
1939. War or no war, he said he felt the time had come when
he should return to Scotland and try to help the young
independent painters, if there were any! So we even cut short
our holiday in the paradise of the Cap, to get back to London
to pack up there as well.

Fergus was quite definite that he would settle in Glasgow
—because it was the most Highland city (he said Edinburgh
was a suburb of London!)—so after forty years, he returned
like the salmon to Scotland.

SCOTLAND 1939~1961

In 1939 when we eventually got to Glasgow, I was able to stay at my school in Blythswood Square, where two of my teachers were resident. Fergus got a room at a new modern hotel near Charing Cross (now part of Strathclyde University) where he was very comfortable. He started to look for a studio, having first contacted Eric de Banzie whom he had known before the first world war. At once Eric and Stella said we must come and stay with them, and we did, most gratefully, until we had found 4 Clouston Street and decided at once it was the ideal flat. On the top floor of the corner house on Queen Margaret Drive, with windows on two sides, the views from it over the Botanic Gardens to the hills beyond were lovely. And in those days it was wonderfully peaceful, no noise of traffic at all.

As so often happens when a husband—or a wife—is an invalid and a constant anxiety, the other outlives the partner by several years. This happened in the case of Ressich. He had been warned his own heart was not too strong, but Lily was constantly ailing and having slight heart attacks, so he was always trying to save her—but Ressich himself succumbed in the mid-thirties, and Lily outlived him two or three years.

Fergus and I were deeply indebted to them both. Of course Ressich left everything to Lily, but when she died she left £2,000 to Fergus, which was wonderful and enabled us to get the Clouston Street flat (which I still have), clean, whitewash the walls and live very carefully for several years.

At this time Patrick Dollan was the Lord Provost of Glasgow and I wrote to him saying that Fergus was returning to live in Scotland, hoping to help young artists who wanted a free and independent art. I also told him of my school where we could start a club for amateurs, and that I would like to hold a meeting in the Commercial College Hall. He replied at once that he would be delighted to take the chair at our meeting and would do all he could to support us— and he did. The meeting was well attended and we enrolled a number for the Celtic Ballet Club—mostly girls, but quite a few men, among them Tom MacDonald, Willison Taylor and William MacLellan. I started the classes the very next week.

Alexander Watt, son of a then well-known painter Fides Watt, sent weekly articles to the British Press, and I quote from an article of Sandy's I came across recently:

> Fergusson returned to Scotland in 1939 and, along with his wife, Margaret Morris, the talented dancer and founder of the world-wide Margaret Morris System of Remedial Aesthetic Movement, became the focal personalities who had the effect of drawing together in Glasgow a group of creative people, including Erik Chisholm the composer, Hugh MacDiarmid the poet, William MacLellan the publisher, Andrew Taylor Elder and many other painters.
>
> The Celtic Ballet was formed in 1940 by Margaret Morris and some fine work was produced in the next two years, including ballets by Chisholm and Stuart Finlay, Fergusson being artistic director. The New Art Club was formed shortly after by this group and Fergusson was elected

President. He continued to hold this position, giving encouragement, sympathy and advice to young painters and hardly missing a meeting. Monthly exhibitions of paintings were held in the Club premises from 1940 and the painters have had recognition from critics throughout the country as the New Scottish Group. They seem destined to carry on the Glasgow School–Hunter Fergusson line of the colourist tradition in Scottish painting.

The war years were good for Glasgow artistically because many foreigners came there. Jankel Adler and Josef Herman made a great contribution and were very stimulating; Dr. Friedlander gave interesting talks on Jerusalem and others came from Glasgow University to open discussions.

I reproduce Fergus's foreword to the book on The New Scottish Group, published by William McLellan in 1947;

Glasgow at the beginning of the War (1939) had no place where an independent artist without money could show his work. The only place to send to was the Glasgow Institute.

The old Art Club with an entrance fee, a yearly subscription of eight guineas, and a committee that refused to admit anyone they did not consider an important artist, was of course out of the question for an artist without money, or a student, however talented. A private show in a dealer's gallery cost one pound a day, and printing expenses.

This state of things was apparently accepted as quite in order, or inevitable; some of us thought it wasn't, and decided to do something about it. So we arranged a meeting which was held in the School of Art, not as inappropriate a place as it would seem, for the architect of the school, Charles Rennie Mackintosh, was one of the greatest and most independent artists Scotland has produced.

We had quite a big meeting, and after a lot of discussion it was agreed that there should be a 'New Art Club', and Marie de Banzie, the first Secretary, was asked to find a room.

After a thorough search, she reported she could find nothing and those of us with experience of such difficulties, thought the usual thing had happened—the defeat of the independent artist. But Andrew Taylor Elder had an inspiration, and acted on it at once. It is to him the New Art Club is indebted for its start—he asked the proprietor of 'Jean's' Tea Room to let us a room, and she agreed. We were soon settled and had our first exhibition and discussion on the 1st December, 1940.

It was clearly right that the Club was opened by Mrs Alison Sheppard for she, as Secretary of the Saltire Society, had devoted herself to freedom for Scottish art, and had already done great things to prepare the way.

The Club subscription was fixed at one pound a year, and one shilling for each picture hung; there was to be a permanent exhibition changed every month; no selecting committee; each member had a right to have anything he sent hung, without interference, unless there wasn't sufficient space. There was a discussion every Wednesday and Sunday, a free discussion of any subject.

Quite recently I had to fulfil an engagement, for a reading of 'My Galsworthy Story' at the Literature Festival at Ilkley. After the performance, a very good-looking Greek lady rushed up to me saying I must come with her to see a friend who was bedridden. He had met Fergus and had two letters from him, which he would like to give me! Of course I could not resist that offer, and agreed to go with this lady at 10 o'clock the next morning. She called for me in a beautiful car and took me to a nursing home where, in a private room sitting up in bed, David Anderson held court. His name will be well remembered in Press circles as Editor of the Mail and the Record in Glasgow; but what not many people know is that he was also a good painter—and now it seems his paintings are all sold!

Anderson is a handsome elderly man, his hair is still dark and his personality forceful. It seems that Eric de Banzie, at

his request, arranged a meeting at the Central Hotel; and Anderson also told me how he kept a tiny corner of the newspaper offices free, for the use of any writer he thought had ideas—Ressich did many of his 'Something I Want to Say' series for the Record, in that tiny corner.

This is one of the letters he gave me:

Glasgow, 18th August, 1942.

My dear Anderson,

Your very good letter deserved to be replied to sooner, but I've had the joiners, plasterers and painters in. I like to think of you having done what Neil Munro would have liked you to do—you remember—'a Hunter's fare is all I would be craving'. That's why years ago I decided to come back to the highlands. I didn't decide to come back on account of the war, but when I thought of the state of art in Scotland, I decided Glasgow was the place where I might do something to help, or try. What Gainsborough said was said also by Sir George Reid, when he felt himself being made a slave to portrait painting, with the results we know. John Lavery had the same regrets. You did a great deal when you were in Glasgow to help Scotland, and that's why I wrote to you. No, I certainly don't want you to get into Art Politics, but you can't help being on the side of <u>freedom</u>. The young people are very much on <u>colour</u>, and with a freedom even the Glasgow School hadn't, but they also insist on freedom in form which hasn't dawned on Scotland. Here they still have the idea that form can be exactly measured by calipers, foot-rules, photography—or anatomical comparison.

You might not like things done by the present generation, but you must allow their right to express themselves <u>honestly</u> and without considering such 'Blimp' institutions as the R.A., the R.S.A. and the Institute, all the same kind of thing —you know all about the workings of these Blimpstitutions. I am constantly talking about the Glasgow School quality of paint, colour, but not as things separate from form, or controlled by photographic or anatomical form.

I never show anybody anything till a year or more after I've done it. The question seems to be whether you have some objective standard and who do you not want to show your things to—do you mean you wouldn't show them to me? That would be strange. I show my things because I feel sure that there are a good many people interested in an honest to God statement, even if they don't agree with my personal point of view. I have lived by this, made a living I mean by this belief for an ordinary lifetime, and I want to help all people willing to try it. I'm not going to help anyone trying to make fame money, or anything, by accepting standards that we both know are either stupidly hypocritical, or dishonest—but I'm getting long, as usual.

Yes, I was in Paris and was part of what you call the 'heroic period', and it has started, including quality, tone, colour, form and mystery. Well I like to think of you in your garden. I have a great respect for Monet, and was at the 'vernissage' of his frond lilies at Durand Ruel's, where Degas seemed to be explaining to him that they hadn't sufficient drawing (showing the academic standard)—

Well, all our best wishes to you and hope nothing disturbs your peace.

Yours very sincerely,

J. D. Fergusson.

I think it was MacLellan who took Fergus and me to see Erik Chisholm. He had composed a ballet 'The Forsaken Mermaid' and played us some of the music. We were enchanted with it. There were only three main characters, but lots of fisher girls and fisher men, mermaids and sea creatures, which made it a possibility for an amateur group. Of course we would need money for costumes, printing etc., and Dollan suggested we ask Sir John Stirling Maxwell of Pollock House to let us give a fête in the grounds with a performance on his lovely lawns. This he readily agreed to, and he said we could use the estate at any time for rehearsals or photographs—which we did. I am glad to think Sir John got some fun out of it, for he followed us around in his wheel-chair. The day of the fête a large crowd gathered, but the sky was overcast—we had hoped for the sun and had carefully placed it behind the audience! Instead it started to rain. Dollan was splendid, he put up his umbrella and refused to leave till the dancers *had* to give up—their clothes were sticking to them!

William Crosbie did some wonderful designs for another ballet by Erik Chisholm, a big one, 'The Earth Shapers'. It was produced at the Theatre Royal and Crosbie was most helpful throughout.

Fergus felt that the Celtic peoples of the Western world were the most creative—perhaps because most closely linked with the East, their trek having been from the mountains of India, along the Mediterranean coast to Spain, then North through France to Ireland and Britain. I quote Fergus on Celtic design:

Since Edinburgh days, I have been interested in Celtic design—made aware of it, perhaps not surprisingly, by a man called Ross who was an enthusiast on it. But pressure of trying to learn to use oil paints and watercolours, fortunately prevented me from being too much interested in the monkish abstractions that have been considered all that could be done and—like everything else in art at the time—something that could be copied but not used, or interfered with in any way. Art was a thing that <u>had been done</u>, and it was for modern artists to copy as well as they could, what was called authentic work. This word is still used to mean 'genuine'; and as all Celtic art or ornament is chiefly concerned with <u>direction of line</u> and movement, the idea is apparently that <u>movement</u>, expressed in direction of line, belongs to the past—what about Toulouse Lautrec? And that brings up the question— was <u>he</u> not Celtic?

I have always had the greatest respect for Lautrec and can think of no artist of any period in any country, who is even in the same class at using line to express people in movement. His expression of people is like paintings of birds on the wing. Most painting of people is like paintings of stuffed birds—to me, 'stuffed shirts'! (Royal Academy portraits). Consequently, a good caricature or a child's drawing is always more like a person than a photographically, or anatomically correct portrait. Distortion is the natural reaction to the dehumanised painting in which nothing is exaggerated, all is correct and exact. The sitter, still, in a state of fixity, is the old head-holder of the early photographer.

Well, all my training in art was made from people on the wing, in music hall, sailing boats, doing things, never in art schools—and what seemed to me the essential movement, was the lead. This became more and more of an urge in me as I went on, consequently, when in Paris I saw Picasso's portrait of a woman with a guitar in the rue Vignon on an Opening Day in 1907, I was not surprised to find progressions of forms contained, or not, by lines in harmonisation of planes—a complexity of forms instead of the Beaux Arts smoothness, the stuffed bird of the museum usual Celtic continuous line.

Fergus settled to painting again. His studio had plenty of light—four windows; but he had white cotton curtains he could draw if the sun was too strong which didn't happen often! He had several exhibitions over the years, mostly at Annan's Gallery at Charing Cross. One was opened by Professor Boase of the French Department in Glasgow University; another by Lord Boyd Orr—for whom Fergus had a great admiration.

James Bridie proposed Fergus and he was elected an honorary member of the Art Club. Fergus appreciated the compliment, and of course attended the first dinner they gave for him—but he never went again! When Bridie was asked about this he said, "He won't come because there are no women!" How right Fergus was—in the Paris cafés, the women's clothes and hats provided the pictorial interest. He said a roomful of men in their dark suits was too dreary for words.

About this time Dr. Tom Honeyman became director of the Kelvingrove Art Gallery and Museum—this was a great step forward for art in Glasgow. He made the Galleries a place to go in the evenings and each opening of a new show an occasion, though he was much opposed by many of the Corporation for the expense he incurred by offering a cup of tea or coffee free! It's amazing to me how the offer of a cup of coffee—which could be had at home—will draw people out! But it's psychological—just holding a cup in your hand makes a social evening.

Honeyman often came to our discussion evenings at the New Art Club and was always helpful. He opened Fergus's first retrospective exhibition at the McLellan Galleries, and William Power remarked on his speech in a letter to David Anderson. I quote it:

> . . . J. D. Fergusson's recent show in Glasgow was a great event, opened by Honeyman in one of the most brilliant laudatory speeches one had ever heard.

The exhibition was very well covered by the Press. Robins Millar's article in the *Evening Citizen* made three specially good points:

> He has an instinct for the rhythm which makes sense out of a picture just as it informs the shape and meaning of a dance. His pictures and his sculptures seem to move with a musical rhythm.
> There is another strange faculty in him of brooding over an idea. His best picture, *Spring, 1914* of a reclining nude woman,

was sketched in that year but only painted 20 years after. He
has done that frequently. It has brought maturity of con-
ception that makes him a serene poet in paint. Fergusson is
an artist who went looking for the rainbow and came back
with a chunk of it. The trouble is, with that gift, what are
you going to do with it! There is little of it in Scotland,
especially in the heart.

1950 was quite an eventful year. In February–March Fergus
had an exhibition at the *Institut Français* in Edinburgh. He
called it 'Paintings of France and Scotland', and always said
it was one of the exhibitions he enjoyed most. It was opened
by the French Ambassador and the whole ambience was
wonderful. The rooms are beautifully proportioned; everyone seemed delighted and several pictures were sold (though
a nice thing about the Institut is that being an official body
they do not mind whether pictures are sold or not).

In June of that year Fergus received the honorary LL.D.
from Glasgow University. He was very happy about this,
because by then he felt that he 'belonged to Glasgow', and
appreciated the honour they were doing him. Also, he hoped
it would strengthen his position in helping the young Scottish
painters. Actually I am not sure it did. Some thought he had
joined the establishment, and that the way the 'New Art
Club' was run was too conventional! He always recognised
that such things as cleaning the premises, or serving tea and
coffee, *must be organised*—but that the artist should be free to
paint what he liked and have it exhibited. "Put your freedom
in your painting", he said.

At the end of June we had a letter from Rita John (who
took us, you remember, to visit Jo Davidson) saying her
mother had died, and she was living in the villa at Golf Juan
—would we come and stay with her? She had a small car
and we could go and bathe at the Château des Enfants. The
offer was irresistible but we were faced with the ordeal of a

continuous night and day journey to Antibes. We were glad that a great friend of ours, Isabel Jeayes, who had worked with me for many years was able to meet us in London— our first time there since 1939. The journey across London was frustrating. After dull self-service cups of tea, breakfast at Lyons Corner House and depositing luggage at Victoria, we had to wander the adjacent streets until time for the Dover train.

This began our annual visits to France, but in future we had no tiring wait in London because two old pupils of mine who lived in Buckingham Gate, Nina Hosali and Gladys Moseley, very kindly asked us to their flat for breakfast and rest. Nina is a painter and Fergus was interested in seeing her new work each year, and in discussing art and philosophy.

Fergus was longing to see Paris again, so we stopped there on our way home, but as we feared, found it terribly changed. The Boul' Miche was hardly recognisable with French student restaurants being replaced by self-service places, and every other shop now selling expensive shoes or clothes. The baker's shop that had never shut for many of the hundred years since Haussmann built the Boulevard St. Michel itself, was still there; but the café d'Harcourt, where Fergus got so much pictorial inspiration, was now a very good, but most respectable bookshop!

Fergus was particularly interested, however, to meet a Polish sociologist, Victor Zoltowski, and Jean Geddes who was helping him with his research, because Zoltowski's work was concerned with 'rhythm': the rhythms in history, and in intellectual and artistic creation. Fergus had always been interested in the relationship of the sciences and the arts, and in rhythm in his painting and sculpture. He often said how sorry he was that the contact with Victor was so brief, but never forgot his comment, "La vie est dure, mais elle est belle". Happily Jean Geddes, who was a painter as well as a

writer, came back to live in Glasgow two years later, and the relationship was renewed.

In 1952 Fergus had a letter from a Mrs. Ian Robertson in Edinburgh, saying she had been told that Fergus, before he left Edinburgh for Paris, had painted a portrait of her father and if he still had it, could she come and see it. I give her own account of what followed:

I had written to him after my father's death to ask if he knew the whereabouts of his portrait of my father painted when they were both very young men, because I hoped to acquire it if I could. He answered me at once saying that he had the portrait, and inviting me to go and see him at Clouston St. Glasgow. My father and he had met as students before the turn of the century and had become friends. 'The finest talker I ever knew' my father said of him—high praise from a man who did not bear bores gladly. The portrait, painted 'for practice' about this time, was exhibited in London, and my grandmother, having contrived a visit there to see it, was highly displeased with it. My father, amused, tried to explain to her that it was not a conventional portrait, just a painting of a young man for which he had been the sitter. Eventually he and J. D. Fergusson left Edinburgh, my father for the Sudan and Egypt and the painter for France. They corresponded, mostly to arrange meetings in France where they went to hear and see Yvette Guilbert together, wrestled together as a form of healthy exercise, and talked and talked. But the difficulties of meeting—including two world wars—finally parted them.

The second world war separated me from my father also, so the meeting and the portrait held special significance for me—an old friendship might tell me something of the past. The friendship was shown to me at once. My husband and I went together and were welcomed warmly. I was at first nervously aware of being looked over and hoped that some resemblance to my father might be seen in me. For my part I saw a most handsome elderly man wearing a pale blue overall as if he had just at that moment stopped painting (which he probably had). He looked like a professional painter. He also looked kind, firm and perceptive. (Later on I was to see that in his habits he was meticulously neat, tidy and well organised and this gave him the time to be always ready to listen and ready to encourage.) We had come by an early afternoon train, but it was late before the portrait was produced. Fergus told me that my father had just come in to see him wearing an overcoat and cap—caps were fashionable and every young blood had one—and he had just painted him in it. The painting was unframed and had a hole from which it once hung on a nail. The young man in it was indeed wearing an overcoat and cap, and a creamy coloured scarf. I could not say it was like my father, but I couldn't say it wasn't like him either, and it struck me that he looked like an amalgam of my father and his immediate family, none of whom Fergus had met but of whom he had caught the basic features. . . .

I wanted to buy the portrait, but Fergus said decisively that I ought to have it and therefore it was mine. It was a most handsome present and I was prepared to take it away there and then. I could not do that, he said, it would have to have its face washed, having lain around for some fifty years. He would wash it, he said, with the best toilet soap! He would then varnish it, have a frame made for it in the way he liked and then I could come and take it away. The day I got the portrait home I inserted a note in the back of the frame recording the gift.

Fergus and I were both delighted with Anne, she combined charm with obvious intelligence and we became great friends. Fergus liked Ian as much as Anne—we spent several happy weekends with them in Edinburgh, though Fergus usually refused to go anywhere under two months!

In 1957 at Antibes, when Fergus's appreciation of the female form was as keen as ever, there was a very lovely young girl who bathed near us in a scant bikini. I spoke to her, explaining my husband was a painter and that he admired her tremendously. She offered at once to pose for him on the beach and he made drawings. She also came to our rooms so that Fergus could draw her head—he called her 'Magnolia' and she was the inspiration for the last picture Fergus painted. If she ever sees this book I hope she will take this as a tribute.

It was Rita, as I have said, who got us to the south after the war, and at this point I feel I must jump back a few years, to her second period in London. She had come from Australia to study acting in London and eventually played several leading parts. Years later she received a considerable legacy from Australia and at once decided to go into management! She took a small narrow house in Park Street, Mayfair, where she could entertain. For a long time she had been a real enthusiast of Fergus's painting and had bought some of his best pictures—when we went to lunch with her in this house, Fergus was enchanted—on each floor there was one room that went through to the back: dining-room on the ground floor, drawing-room on the first, and her bedroom on second. In each room she had just *one* of Fergus's pictures, over the mantelpiece, and no others. Each room had been decorated to harmonise with the picture and also to show it up to the best advantage—walls, floors, curtains, chairs etc. As she had excellent taste, the effect was quite wonderful.

When Rita went to live with her mother at Golf Juan, she sold most of her pictures, but she took a fairly recent one with her and hung it in her own room until her mother died. I quote now what Fergus wrote on going to the 'Florentine' in 1958:

> Back to the 'Florentine', having my petit dejeuner under the arbour, seeing another point of view about the wisteria leaves and blossom I didn't expect to find at this time of the year. A dull day exactly like the West coast of Scotland's weather, most delightfully soft, warm, damp air. The cat has gone to sleep, Meg gone to bathe, and strangely enough my mind is on Rimsky Korsakoff's 'Hymn to the Sun'.
>
> Last night we had a perfect dinner prepared by old Claudine—chicken, crepes, Beaumol cheese, good wine, and all the time looking at my picture 'Eastra', hymn to the sun, which my hostess bought at my show at the Lefèvre Gallery when in St. James's, I think in 1936. This is a picture of a head I made in polished brass—all polished like a door-knob, in <u>pure brass</u>—of the Saxon Goddess of Easter—representing the triumph of the sun after the gloom of winter. Below it is a very rich collection of fruit, an attempt to express the hoped-for fertility of the coming year. The head is composed entirely of sections of a sphere—the forehead is round, the eyes are round, cheeks round, hair represented by two pads,

one on each ear, half-spheres, cheeks; all the same idea; the fruit is a continuation of the fullness and, by them, of the brass head—which is the effect of the sun. The neck looks quite like a woman, but is not, in the ordinary sense, in the least anatomically correct. This picture I have seen in the house often before, but it has recently been changed to the dining-room, where it is placed above the sideboard. Below it is a huge wooden bowl full of fruit, repeating the fruit in the picture, and so expresses wonderfully the real sympathy the owner of a picture can show for the work of an artist. He probably put everything he knew and felt and thought of into it, but took it for granted that no one would see what he was trying to express—or care if they did.

What's all that got to do with it?—The Saxons' Easter, fertility, the right frame and hung in the right place. Art is not Saxon, but in this case it seems less justifiable, for the sculptor-painter is not Saxon, and rather or completely the opposite: he's a pure Highland Scotsman, definitely a Celt He still has a great sympathy with Celtic sculpture, and on the Celtic crosses there are 'bosses'—round shapes, half-spheres which express for him 'Suns', fullness, open eyes, women's breasts, apples, peaches, health and overflow— something to give, and depending on the Sun for its ripeness and usefullness. Sounds far fetched, no doubt, but not to the man who did the brass head and the painting of it and the fruit—apparently not to the person who owns the picture.

After three days at Antibes, thunder, lightning, mistral and rain—think of Rimsky's 'Hymn to the Sun'. My composer.

Fergus and I were both very happy at the 'Florentine'. The arbour where we ate our breakfast and dinner was a constant delight—looking over the sea to the Cap; the changing light at sunset and then the stars in a dark sky, with much interesting talk to go with it all. But we neither of us liked the hair-raising drives to the Cap each day. Our hostess was a wonderful driver and claimed she had never had an accident, but there were plenty of near shaves as the dents on the car testified! So sometimes Fergus would spend the whole day sitting in the arbour under a very old wistaria tree. He said he had to move his chair quite often, because the tendrils from the wistaria were constantly looking for something to curl round (you can actually *see* them move); they would wind round Fergus's neck and wrists!—till he felt they would hold him there forever.

Among the many letters Fergus received in the south, were some from the Glasgow painter, Donald Bain. I give an extract from one of them which amused us:

> Dear Fergus,
>   . . . What do you think, a large turtle was caught in the Clyde, and another one washed ashore in the Solway . . .
>   Michonze had a show in Adam's gallery, London, in July. I had a note from him, he writes—
>   'Oh life, oh painting—la misère de l'artiste. Sold a few 'pitchers' and we have to go on with the bloody struggle. Never have the proper conditions for work. Bon courage, je t'embrasse vieux pote, et salut à tous . . .'
>   Best wishes, yours aye, Donald.

I now include an unpublished essay which Fergus meant to use in a future book—I think it is the best thing he wrote. For sixteen wonderful years we enjoyed these magical summers at the Château des Enfants, with a beautiful open Renault car and a charming old chauffeur, Marcel at our disposal, which inspired much of the following,

ART AND ATAVISM
THE DRYAD

We were staying with G.D. at the Cap d'Antibes. I was standing in the front porch waiting for Meg—glad to be out of the afternoon sun, and intrigued by the definitely mechanical design of the big Renault car. Its mechanical shapes continued logically, even over the bonnet—it was the

only car at that time with sustained and unapologetic
persistence of shapes. Very satisfying. Convincing, so convincing that it threw my mind back to the time when
(about 1908) there was starting in Paris the research after
logic and line and form by Picasso and others—Picasso's
'Portrait of Kahnweiler' and 'The Woman with the Man-
dolin'. This research was taken up later and systematised by
Metzinger and Gleise and became known to the public as
Cubism.

Here, in the cool shade of the porch, I was hypnotised by
the brilliance of the sunlight, watching the changing shapes
caused by the light and reflections on the windscreen and
highly polished body of the car. In the light and in the
shadow of the house, as high in pitch and brilliant as paintings,
the shapes were destroying the actual form of the car and
composing, or re-composing and harmonising themselves;
changing with the movement of foliage, playing with reflections of leaves and bloom of the Rose Laurier—all
qualified by the blue sky—making the solid, metal, mechanical car as fluid in effect as moving water, until I was as
much involved and merged in it all as when I bathed in the
sea in sunlight. In both cases I lose touch with everything but
the association of colour forms, and recollections of the many
attempts I had made in years of painting all sorts of subjects
—landscapes, seascapes, portraits—and of the intense research
to find a means of using these 'could-be-mechanical shapes':
to find the contribution they could make to free emotional
expression.

It was a state very like swimming in the sea in sunlight, in
a gentle breeze, in the very buoyant water of the Mediterranean which removes all consciousness of weight, and
the temperature of the water, like the temperature of the
porch, allows a complete detachment from everything but
thought—a state when some of the mystery of things may
come through and give something to keep us struggling, for
long periods, to find a means of expansion towards that
something we don't understand . . . Meg arrives. The car

whirrs off down the drive into the deep shadows of the trees; glints and splashes of sunlight coming through them; out on the main road, purring and murmuring in the blaze of sun — the open car gives no protection.

Marcel likes speed. We don't like speed, but we like the rush of cool air in the shadows of the big eucalyptus trees. Past the roadside café of the Beau Site, shutters down for the heat; glad we're not in the bus, hot and crowded, crashing along. What a wonderful thing a good car is — nearly flying, as easy as swimming. How right this perfect, apparently effortless, mechanical movement is: the sharp cleanness of it, true harmony, like a flash of light on the windscreen as we round a corner — harmonising with the movement of the driver as he swings the wheel. It's wonderful. Yes. Clean-cut angular shapes, even curves should be made up of clean-cut angular shapes at high speed. Roundness and fullness seem too easy, too lazy, not alive enough.

It all seems right: the wonderful feeling of ease; the rush of fresh air in the heat of the afternoon; speed creating a coolness that allows the detachment necessary to enjoy wonderful hot sunlight. How fortunate to live in a period when mechanism is so highly developed that it attunes itself, harmonises with and becomes part of an atmosphere of acceleration, which gives to an ordinary journey a feeling of spiritual adventure — instead of a-walking along in the heat, perspiring, dusty and thirsty, thinking of the weight of things you will have to carry back from your shopping; or bumping along behind a patient, perspiring horse, regretting that he should have to be on the dusty road instead of under a tree in the shade — wondering if he is suffering so, merely because you are shopping.

Round the corner and there's a stretch of blue sea and the mountains through the eucalyptus trees; white horses on the sea, white triangles of yachts' sails glint as the fresh breeze deepens the blue of the water; then the town, more cars, more mechanisation, more glittering, highly polished motor bodies and bright coloured cars everywhere, wonderful cars

—hard to cross the road; we get out to go to the old town
square. Down the narrow street, always having to get onto
the pavement to make room for a car. Not so agreeable when
you're not in them these cars, damn them.

Well, here, the old square—the town hall, post office, café,
everything. How calm and peaceful, if these dam'd cars
weren't continually nearly running you down. The road
should be left to walk on in this restful old square. The smell
of absinthe is refreshing and the sight of ice is a relief—
anyway the trees are very beautiful, bright and casting cool
shadows. It's interesting stuff to paint: the white house and
grey gable, emerald green shutters and the high plantan tree.
They're interesting these plantans; the branches are wonderful where the bark is off and they are almost flesh colour.
Well, I'll wait for Meg under this one—it's very high, looking
up into it; the way the branches compose is amazing,
fascinating; what a wonderful thing a tree is. It's strange,
mysterious, isn't it? So settled, quiet, serene. It's so old, so full
of time, it gives the feeling that it has always been there, or
somewhere. It's just a tree and just taking its time; the shade
it is making seems to be part of it; it doesn't flash or scintillate
this old plantan, it accepts its friend the sun and absorbs it;
with it, makes beautiful patterns on the branches, the trunk,
the ground—wonderful. There is form, colour, depth, shade,
dignity, friendliness, protection, comfort—yes, all that, but
there's something else we get, beyond these things that we see
and feel—there's something else, a tremendous lot more.
Then we just stand still and look and see nothing; something
is happening slowly ... and Meg suddenly says—'I've done
all that.' She has done her shopping. I wonder if I can get
some blue webbing for a belt, and two galvanized rings for
a buckle. So we leave the old Place and the plantan.

Yes, trees are wonderful things. Perhaps the Druids were
right. Oh yes, of course they were right, marvellously right.
Dru, dous, Druid—yes of course, that is what is in the tree to
the person in sympathy, but how can I be in sympathy?—In
the mechanical age, cars everywhere. For the person aware of

progress and open to modern impressions and modern thought, trees must be out of date perhaps, but I don't feel that. I've always liked trees; my father tried hard to interest me in them, to know them by name and to realise how beautiful they were. As a boy I was more interested in bicycles and speed. My father belonged to what Burns calls 'Clans frae the wuds'—clans from the wooded part of the highlands (not like Barra, where Peploe said there was only one tree). My father's people had lived for generations, perhaps more than a thousand years, among trees and I have painted and drawn them all my life, wherever I went; but the real contact was with the plantan in the old square at Antibes.

When I got back to London I went to the wood-yard and bought a batten, four inches square, seven feet long. With the idea of the plantan still in my mind I drew two intertwined lines on one side, like the movement of the branches. I put it in the corner of the room where I could see it nearly all the time. It stood there for about two years, I couldn't get a start on it.

One day the bell rang, I went down, opened the door and found old Toshie—Charles Rennie Mackintosh—with a delightful happy smile, holding a small flower pot with two slim, intertwined twigs, two leaves near the bottom and two more at the top. He laughed and said—'I saw this on a barrow and had to bring it to you, it's so like you.' What a charming thing to do and how amazingly sympathetic—real sympathy! I hadn't seen him for some time. We talked and I was delighted with the plant, which seemed to him quite in order— and it was. Delightful old man, I always had the greatest admiration for him and his work, long before I knew him. When he left I sat looking at the twined twigs. They seemed to remind me of something, I could not remember what. I started to make a careful drawing of the movement and the plane relation of the leaves. As I went on I began to feel I had done it before—you know the feeling. I made a bigger drawing on two sheets of paper and stuck them together very complete. I felt I had fixed it and put it aside. Then one day, long after, I noticed the pencil lines on the side of the batten—they were just like Toshie's plant.

I began to think again of sculpting the batten and I came back to the plantan—the movement of the branches, the roundness like the roundness of a nude; then the words 'dou', 'drus', dryad came back to my mind and I had the idea at once of a dryad, with the movement and form created by the twig of Toshie's plant. I went out and bought two chisels, put the batten on the.table and started with the leaf motif at the feet, going to the legs. As I worked on the legs in the ivory coloured wood, I again got the feeling of having done it before, or that I had seen it before—but I had never before seen a sculpture like the one I had in mind. I could not trace it. It kept in my mind but I worked on, without being able to remember the connection. Then my mind wandered to Glasgow and to wandering round the museum at Kelvingrove and I remembered a set of bagpipes. Instead of the usual mechanical turning, they looked as if they had been carved, made round, by hand and of ivory. My sculpture was like them.

I completed the dryad and sent it to the Scottish Group show with Peploe and Hunter at the Leicester Gallery. Sickert wrote the preface to our catalogue and in his usual acutely perceptive and charming style, he said—'The Dryad is the best use a four-inch batten has been put to in recent times.' Coming from Sickert it pleased me, for I have the same respect for him that I have for Mackintosh—both were genuine artists from the start to the finish. Some other critic, knowing that I didn't usually do sculpture, said that it had even 'remarkable skill.' I quote this because it leads to the question—how could I have had any technical skill in my first wood carving?

Well, once when I was very young and very revolutionary, I started to tell my father about my modern ideas and how antiquated these highland ancestors he was always telling me about seemed to me to be. He was a kind old man and

listened patiently as usual, then said—'John, you've never heard of your grand-uncle the wheelwright,' and then told me about the great skill of this man. He seemed to be able to do anything with wood; was a free-thinker in the fullest sense—at that time a terrible thing in the highlands. Anyone applying to him for a job was given an axe and a piece of wood, and told to make a tree nail, on the stone step. If he hit the step he was no good; if he succeeded, no credentials were asked for. The grand-uncle was tremendously strong, had fought a professional pugilist, and was confident he could keep his employees in order—or throw them out.

As an enthusiast at that time on strength and boxing, I soon realised that my own revolutionary ideas were pale and rather intellectual compared with the very living ones of this ancestor—but my dryad <u>was</u> free-thinking and was strong, not an attempt to conform with anything but my feeling about trees and the spirit of them. The grand-uncle was a kind and very much loved man, very human. My dryad was meant to be very human and was intended to express both love for trees and the desire to be human—the desire to be free. People couldn't understand why the dryad had well developed breasts—too human, they said. I think my dryad had all the characteristics of my grand-uncle—love of trees, love of wood, free thought, free expression, human sympathy and, as the critic said, considerable technical skill.

The dryad was no doubt founded on the bagpipes in Kelvingrove Gallery. All my life I liked the bagpipes, if I hadn't I wouldn't have looked for them. If I had not been a Scot and Highland, would I have thought of the pipes? The fellow, the sculptor that carved these pipes was probably of a 'clan frae wuds'. Highlanders loved trees and wood—old Toshie was of course a Highlander, how do we know how near me atavistically? I know how near he was as a friend, and his little flower-pot from the barrow in London with its twining twigs is a traditional Celtic sculpture movement.

Tradition generally merely means something that has been handed down ready-made and in a definitely fixed form—

any interference with which is, to the traditionalist, not to be tolerated on any account. And most people think you should be like your parents—the more like the better. That idea cannot be accepted by anyone concerned with anything creative—the artist, for example. Tradition, to me, is a racial characteristic that is always going on, kept alive by the creative person's contribution; and those contributing may join the mainstream, if the artist is free enough from the obfustications of actuality to be able to take his time, and to discipline himself to an awareness and readiness for the moment when he may get the chance to transmit some of the mystery of life, which goes to make a tradition. In this way he may help to keep his race alive and make a contribution to it, to his country and consequently to the world.

Tradition, to me, is the spirit of the race, or nation, which is always there and ready to help, as long as it is kept alive and nourished by creative contributions. Heredity is generally accepted because it is considered to be sane life, reasonable and does not seem to go too far back.

Atavism, I find, is generally looked on as vague and retrograde, having no visible continuity like the supposed continuity of the calendar—one year after another, one generation after another. So all this about the Druid may seem very far fetched, and by calendar time is far fetched. But as someone said the other night—'perhaps the truth is far fetched'. Anyway, by using an account of what happened to me, I have attempted to explain what I mean by atavism.

When we got back to Glasgow, Fergus was thinking of how we could widen the scope of our 'New Art Club' where we held monthly exhibitions of members' work to encourage more freedom in art outside our group. He suggested we hold exhibitions where our members could invite artists outside the group to exhibit, and it might be called 'Artists I admire'.

Jean Geddes was then living in Glasgow; she had returned to look after her mother and had found an old laundry

behind the Hyndland Road which made an excellent studio.
Fergus had gone there several times some years before, and
was much interested in a series of pictures she was doing of
'Picts', so he wrote her the following letter:

4 Clouston Street, Glasgow, N.W.   14th January, 1960.
Dear Jean,
    I hope to see you at the party on January 26th. As you
will see by the invitation, a picture exhibition is announced.
I have agreed to invite 'Some of the painters I admire' and I
would very much like to have one or two of your paintings
—I don't mind if they have been exhibited before. We want
to make a really good show, the room has been re-decorated
so the pictures will be well presented.
    The idea is to ask different artists to invite others to exhibit
under the heading 'Some painters I admire' and it is hoped in
this way that these premises, which are so central, may further
modern painting in Glasgow. Please let me know by phone
or card if you can accept my invitation.

Very sincerely yours,
Fergus.

Exhibition at 299 West George Street, Glasgow C.2.
Opening Tuesday, 26th January, 1960.

In 1954 I had taken the *Celtic Ballet of Scotland* to Ted
Shawn's Summer School in the Berkshire hills. All my friends
thought we were really launched—but all that came of it
was that my best dancers got jobs in big musicals, before they
landed in England! Bruce McClure was booked by Howard
and Wyndham's; so I had to start training a new company.
    It was Fergus's idea that I might get more support if I called
it *The Scottish National Ballet*, and always included the traditional dances (Highland and Scottish Country) with ballets
based on old Scottish legends as well as modern themes. So
this we did—in 1960. Kenneth Ireland offered us a special
show at Pitlochry to launch it. Of course Fergus came with
us. After the performance when we were having tea in the
garden by the theatre, a small woman with grey hair came
to our table and said to Fergus—'I salute you as a great
member of our clan!' Fergus stood up, saying—'Excuse me

but who are you?' When the reply came—'Marjorie
Fergusson of Baledmund,' he was overwhelmed. To his
father and mother (both Perthshire Fergussons), Baledmund
was much more important than Buckingham Palace!

Mrs. Fergusson said we must come and stay with her at
Baledmund as the annual clan gathering was to be held there
the next day. To my amazement, Fergus at once agreed! If
we stayed two more nights at Pitlochry, it meant we would
only have one night in Glasgow before leaving for France—
our tickets were booked and Fergus usually insisted on two
days peace for final packing. But as my grandmother used
to say—'circumstances alter cases, as broken noses alter faces'.

Fergus had been charmed by Marjorie Fergusson, and also
by Meg Fergusson, wife of Finlay Fergusson, Laird of
Pitlochry, who fetched us from Elizabeth Fergusson's
cottage. She was a second cousin of Fergus's with whom
we were staying. When I expressed my surprise at Fergus's
ready agreement, he explained again about Baledmund being
the seat of the Perthshire Fergussons.

We had a wonderful time. Sir James and Lady Fergusson
were also staying there for the Gathering and he was a sincere
admirer of Fergus's work. He had opened an exhibition for
him at Ayr, and said at the time how much he admired a
particular picture but could not afford it. We later stayed a
week with them at Kilkerren and saw the wonderful
vegetable garden; Fergus suggested selling the picture by
barter!—Sir James to send us a basket of vegetables each
week. This was agreed, but soon Sir James wrote that he had
decided to sell the whole vegetable garden—so no barter
was possible.

Remarkable to relate, it was a wonderfully sunny day for
the Gathering and Fergus enjoyed it immensely. There was
piping and Gaelic singing and a grand tea—it was quite a
memorable day.

1960 was Fergus's last summer at Antibes. For the past two years the Château bathing had not been available, so we had taken rooms nearer to Antibes and the Garoupe beach. One had to wade through seaweed to get to deep water. Fergus was quite active, but I noticed he did not stride out as strongly as he used to on the quite long walk to the beach. He swam as easily as ever, but lay longer on the towels we spread between the rocks.

One day on the Cap we met Hamish Lawrie, a young painter Fergus admired, and his wife Sheena, with their son Kenneth, then a small boy. Hamish had a camera and wanted to group us together. We were arguing about who should be out and take the photo, when a charming American who happened to be passing, said, "Let me take the photograph,

then you can all be in it", and he did. It is the last in which
Fergus and I are together.

Though as always we hated leaving the sun and the south,
our return to London was brightened by the prospect of the
celebrations of the 50th anniversary of the Margaret Morris
Movement, of which Fergus was the Art Director. Isabel
Jeayes had organised this jubilee. There was a big demonstra-
tion with pupils from all over Britain and from abroad; a
picture exhibition to which Fergus had contributed opened
by Lady Norton; photographs and press cuttings from 1910
to 1960 collected by Isabel; and an evening reception in Park
Lane, at which Fergus was delighted to meet many old
friends. He was much moved by the appreciation shown by
teachers and students past and present. Then Phyllis Calvert

made a quite wonderful speech and presented gifts. It was a most happy evening and Fergus seemed none the worse for it; but it was his last public appearance.

On the train back to Glasgow, though Fergus was most anxious to be in the Clouston Street flat, his thoughts turned again to Antibes and the wonders of it, so I give one of his notes after this last visit—

> Antibes.
>
> One of the most evident effects of this visit to Antibes, is the return to Robert Burns. I felt this when I first came in 1913, but did not so clearly realise that the sympathetic climate and surroundings give one liking—you get into a state that allows you to like people, flowers, skies, leaves, nearly everything natural and simple. The walk round the ramparts, very old ladies sitting on their doorsteps, all seem in order—no evident pressure.
>
> > 'Freedom is a nobele thing
> > it gives man liking.'
> > Barbour.

In Glasgow, again, at last, Fergus's one idea was to get back to his painting. About two years before, someone had left him a large canvas (about 6′ × 4′) and he had started to sketch in two female figures, suggesting the spirit of the magnolia trees which he watched and loved every summer in the south. One year we had a room opening onto a garden with a magnificent magnolia in front of our window, so Fergus made many studies of the flowers. The buds are pure white, becoming cream as they open fully, and just before they fade they are the colour of warm skin—not sun-tanned. Fergus made many many studies of them, some with colour notes, also sketches for the large picture he was going to paint.

Here, I feel I must mention the dog that attached himself to Fergus. Luckily he was not a stray, but a large well-fed Alsatian belonging to the proprietors of the house. Neither

Fergus nor I liked a ground-floor room, because we wanted lots of fresh air, but didn't like night visitors! So we put chairs across the french window to try to discourage them. This dog must have been very sensitive, for he could easily have jumped over the chairs, but he never did. He slept outside across our window. As soon as Fergus was at his breakfast, when I removed the chairs, the dog bounded in and settled with his head on Fergus's feet. We were very sad to leave him because it had been one of those instinctive friendships between a human and an animal that Fergus appreciated so much.

Fergus was very happy to be back in Glasgow and to continue his magnolia picture. It consisted of two nude female figures, one facing and one back view, surrounded by large magnolia flowers.

Following on the Pitlochry theatre performance, Howard and Wyndhams had booked a tour of no. 1 theatres in Scotland for 1961 — so I was busy all day with rehearsals, and all November and December Fergus worked continuously on his magnolia picture. He made his own porridge for lunch, which he had with a whole pint of Jersey milk because there was a lot of cream on it. I got back in time to do our evening meal which we always had together. My intention was to send the company on tour, and then devote myself to looking after Fergus. We had a charming doctor who came periodically to give Fergus a check-up, though he was never ill. But now the doctor said his blood pressure was on the low side, though he did not seem concerned about it. I find it hard to forgive him for not warning me that *low* blood pressure can be as fatal as high blood pressure; and I encouraged Fergus to rest, whereas now I am told he would have lived much longer if I had kept him moving and given him alcohol.

Maybe it was 'all for the best'. I would not have wanted him to live to be a decrepit old man.

1939–1961

On New Year's Eve of 1961 I saw the new moon through glass! I opened the window and got Fergus to look at it with me, but I was worried. We always started the new year in bed; then Fergus would go out in his dressing gown with cake, wine and a piece of coal. When he knocked on the door I let him in and we partook of a little wine and cake. We never went to a Hogmanay party till this ceremony was completed. The year before, in 1960, we were later than usual and I rang up very old friends who lived below us to ask if their party was still going on. Someone replied, "The party is going strong, but the hostess has gone out and the host passed out". However we went down, and finally the hostess returned and the host revived, so all was well.

Everything still seemed to be all right with Fergus, but though he was walking around, he wanted more and more to lie down and sleep for long periods. I was told he should not be left alone all day, so I got a day nurse, a charming girl that Fergus liked, but I realise now this was my big mistake, making evident to him that he was really ill. He told me once that when his father was ill he said to him, "John, there's a time for disappearing". The next night, when Fergus looked into his father's room, which he always did however late he got home and usually found him asleep, the old man was sitting up in bed. He raised both hands saying, "I'm at the Gates, John!" Fergus took him in his arms but he had already gone.

Fergus's end was very similar and for the same reason I am sure he felt that if he needed to be looked after, it was time 'for disappearing'.

I got back about six one evening and found him asleep in bed, the nurse sitting beside him. He looked perfectly healthy and a good colour, neither pale nor drawn. I took one of his hands in mine and he gave it a firm grip, then relaxed, and the nurse said "I think he's gone", and he had. He never opened his eyes again. To me this was a terrific shock. I thought Fergus would live to a hundred.

We neither of us had any accepted religious beliefs, but we both felt instinctively that the physical body was the least important part, that somehow the spirit, or essence of a person must continue. But we were content to accept that while on this earth one could not know 'how' or 'why'. I feel Fergus is with me now, and in some ways, nearer to me than ever before.

I will end with a quotation from the tribute of an old friend of Fergus's early Paris days, André Dunoyer de Segonzac:

'Ce grand artiste, d'une totale indépendance, a ignoré les formules éphémères du moment et a suivi sa voie durant sa longue et belle vie d'artiste. Son oeuvre subira victorieusement l'épreuve du Temps, car elle est authentique, très vivante et vraie.'

AND AFTER...

In April and May of 1961, Professor Andrew McLaren Young arranged an exhibition of Fergus's water-colours and drawings in the Glasgow University Print Room—thirty-four exhibits. This was very well attended and many things were sold. I was very glad, for Fergus had little to leave me except pictures, but these are now proving a very good investment.

In October-November, the Glasgow Art Gallery held an exhibition of Scottish painting, including sixteen oils by Fergus. In November-December, the Scottish Committee of the Arts Council sponsored a memorial exhibition to tour the art galleries of Scotland. They asked Professor Young to organise the exhibition and do the catalogue—and he certainly made a wonderful job of it. I shall always feel deeply indebted to him.

The exhibition opened at the Diploma Gallery of the Scottish Academy where it was beautifully presented.

In 1962 a Memorial Dinner was arranged for March 9th, Fergus's birthday. It took place at Burlington House, Bath Street, Glasgow. The principal speakers were Sir James Fergusson of Kilkerran, Bart., Hugh MacDiarmid [Christopher M. Grieve], LL.D., John Donald Kelly, C.B.E., Douglas Young, Andrew McLaren Young, Councillor William Brown, Dr. Maurice S. Miller, J.P., Eric de Banzie, Margaret Morris Fergusson. Emilio Coia was in the chair. It was a memorable evening but of course for me it was a great ordeal. The speeches were excellent—I only wish I had them on tape!—Hugh MacDiarmid's was outstanding. I said very little and only just managed not to break down. The Clan Fergusson piper gave his services and we ended on a cheerful note, which I know Fergus approved.

Index

Acknowledgements

The Author and Publisher gratefully acknowledge permission to reproduce material from the following sources: the Charles Rennie Mackintosh Collection of Glasgow University; the literary executors of Katherine Mansfield; the Scottish Arts Review.